RECONSIDERING KNOWLEDGE: FEMINISM AND THE ACADEMY

RECONSIDERING KNOWLEDGE: FEMINISM AND THE ACADEMY

EDITED BY
MEG LUXTON &
MARY JANE MOSSMAN

Fernwood Publishing
Halifax & Winnipeg

Editing: Jessica Antony
Cover Design: John van der Woude
Printed and bound in Canada by Hignell Book Printing

Published in Canada by Fernwood Publishing
32 Oceanvista Lane. Black Point, Nova Scotia, B0J 1B0
and 748 Broadway Avenue, Winnipeg, Manitoba, R3G 0X3
www.fernwoodpublishing.ca

Fernwood Publishing Company Limited gratefully acknowledges the financial support
of the Government of Canada through the Canada Book Fund and the Canada Council
for the Arts, the Nova Scotia Department of Communities, Culture and Heritage,
the Manitoba Department of Culture, Heritage and Tourism under the Manitoba Publishers
Marketing Assistance Program and the Province of Manitoba,
through the Book Publishing Tax Credit, for our publishing program.

Library and Archives Canada Cataloguing in Publication

Reconsidering knowledge : feminism and the
academy / edited by Meg Luxton & Mary Jane Mossman.

Includes bibliographical references.
ISBN 978-1-55266-476-6

1. Feminism and higher education. 2. Feminist theory.
3. Education, Higher. I. Luxton, Meg II. Mossman, Mary Jane

LC197.R43 2012   378.0082   C2011-908401-5

CONTENTS

Acknowledgements 9

Contributor Biographies 11

Introduction: Perspectives and Passions
about Feminism and the Academy 14
    Mary Jane Mossman and Meg Luxton
    Feminism and the Academy: Revealing the "Other" 17
    Feminism and the Academy:
    (Re)Engaging the "Knowledge Revolution" 18
    Feminism and the Academy:
    Remembering History/Recalling Resistance 20
    Concluding Comments 21

Part One
Feminism and the Academy: Revealing the "Other" 23

1. **Feminism and the Academy: Transforming Knowledge?** 24
    Meg Luxton
    Feminist Challenges, Challenging Feminism 24
    Women's Studies: An Interdisciplinary "Discipline" 30
    Feminism, Scholarship and Formal Knowledge in Movement 33
    Conclusions: Why Feminism? Why Women's Studies? 36

2. **Cartographies of Knowledge and Power:**
   Transnational Feminism as Radical Praxis 42
    M. Jacqui Alexander and Chandra Talpade Mohanty
    The U.S. Academy: Mapping Location and Power 45
    The Politics of Feminist Knowledge: Curricular Maps and Stories 49
    Multiplying Radical Sites of Knowledge 56

3. **Sexual Diversity in Cosmopolitan Perspective** 64
    Elisabeth Young-Bruehl
    The Globalization of Sexology and Changes in Its Categories 64
    The Globalization of the Study of Prejudices
    Against Sexual Minorities and Sexuality 66
    Tolerance for Multisexuality in the Globalizing World 69
    Sexual Pathology in Global Context 71

Part Two
Feminism and the Academy:
(Re)Engaging the "Knowledge Revolution"..................................... 75

4. **Universities Upside Down:**
    The Impact of the New Knowledge Economy....................................76
    Margaret Thornton
    Transforming the Academy.. 76
    The Idea of the University.. 77
    Knowledge Reconsidered... 79
    Knowledge Capitalism... 80
    Academic Capitalism and the Remasculinization of the Academy............. 85
    Conclusion... 87

5. **The University-on-the-Ground:**
    Reflections on the Canadian Experience... 96
    Janice Newson
    General Perspective... 99
    Retrenching, Retrofitting and Re-Positioning
    Canadian Universities, 1975-1995 99
    Launching Canadian Universities as Knowledge Businesses
    in the Global Knowledge Industry: 1995 to the Present......................105
    Trouble in the University-on-the-Ground..112
    A Concluding Statement..122

Part Three
Feminism and the Academy:
Remembering History/Recalling Resistance 129

6. **Bluestockings and Goddesses:**
    Writing Feminist Cultural History 130
    Ann Shteir
    Restoring Bluestockings 131
    Elizabeth Carter..134
    Angelica Kauffman 138
    Flora..142
    Concluding Points..144

7. **Feminism, Ecological Thinking and the Legacy of Rachel Carson** ..150
    Lorraine Code
    Rachel Carson and Ecological Thinking...150
    Feminist Epistemology..159
    Conclusion..165

To all the women and men who,
in its first fifty years, made York University
a safe and creative place
where feminist scholarship, teaching and learning
could flourish within a feminist community.

ACKNOWLEDGEMENTS

We are grateful to the administrative staff and committee for the U50 celebrations at York University, which provided the impetus and funding to create the lecture series on which this collection is based. Professor Pina D'Agostino at Osgoode Hall Law School offered help and enthusiasm to the Institute for Feminist Legal Studies to propose this project, and Professor Linda Peake at the Centre for Feminist Research willingly provided excellent initial guidance in submitting the proposal. We appreciate most sincerely their time and support. In recognition of this support, royalties from this publication will be divided equally between the Institute for Feminist Legal Studies and the Centre for Feminist Research.

The lecture series received energetic help from the administrators of our units too: Syed Hussan at the Centre for Feminist Research provided ongoing attention to all the details, and both Joan Shields and then Lielle Gonsalves at the Institute for Feminist Studies at Osgoode offered assistance in publicizing the lectures to the York community. We are also grateful to Professor Ena Dua at the Centre for Feminist Research for her support in ensuring that Chandra Mohanty was able to present her lecture as part of this series.

We also thank the lecturers for their work in revising papers for this collection, and to both Lindsay Gonder, the undergraduate programme secretary of the School of Women's Studies and Sarah Hurowitz, JD 2011, who provided technical and editorial assistance to us in creating the final manuscript for publication.

We especially thank the following authors and journals for their kindness in permitting us to republish revised versions of papers:

> The paper by M. Jacqui Alexander and Chandra Talpade Mohanty is reproduced with the kind permission of the authors and of the editors and publishers of *Critical Transnational Feminist Praxis* (2010).

> Elisabeth Young-Bruehl's paper is reproduced with the kind permission of the author and the editors of *Studies in Gender and Sexuality* (2010). Sadly, the contributors to this book learned of Elisabeth's sudden death in December 2011. Feminist scholarship and activism have lost a significant advocate. She will be missed by all of us.

> Margaret Thornton's paper is a revised version of a paper earlier

published in the *Canadian Journal of Women and the Law* (2010), reproduced with the permission of the author and the *Journal*.

Janice Newson's paper is a revised version of a paper earlier published in the *Puerto Rico Higher Education Research and Information Center
Journal* (2006), and reproduced with the permission of the author
and editor of the *Journal*.

We also want to salute Fernwood Publishing, which has supported
feminist scholarship since its inception in 1991, ensuring that our books get
written, published and read. We thank founder Errol Sharpe and all his co-
workers for their efforts. In particular, we thank Fernwood for its contributions
to this book: Beverley Rach and Debbie Mathers for production, John van
der Woude for the cover design and Jessica Antony for her careful editing.

Finally, we want to acknowledge the important role of Professor Sheila
Embleton who, during her term as Vice-President Academic at York, provided
leadership and impressive support for feminist scholarship in universities
generally and for the School of Women`s Studies at York. In this context, we
also thank our faculty colleagues, staff and students for their support for this
lecture series at York, and for their continuing inspiration to us as feminists.

Meg Luxton and Mary Jane Mossman, Toronto

CONTRIBUTOR BIOGRAPHIES

M. Jacqui Alexander is Cosby Endowed Chair in the Humanities at Spelman College and Professor of Women and Gender Studies at the University of Toronto. Her work has focused extensively on the relations between nationalism and sexuality and on the ways in which heterosexuality works as a verb to organize nation-building projects across both neoimperial and neocolonial formations, illustrated in her recent book, *Pedagogies of Crossing: Meditations on Feminism, Sexual Politics, Memory and the Sacred* (2005). Other recent work has wrestled with the sacred dimensions of experience and the significance of sacred subjectivity. Under the auspices of a Guggenheim fellowship, Dr. Alexander has continued work on the embeddedness of Kongo epistemology within metaphysical systems in the Caribbean.

Lorraine Code is Distinguished Research Professor Emerita in Philosophy at York University and a Fellow of the Royal Society of Canada. She is author of *Epistemic Responsibility* (1987) and *What Can She Know? Feminist Theory and the Construction of Knowledge* (1991). In *Rhetorical Spaces: Essays on (Gendered) Locations* (1995), she addresses incredulity, empathy, relativism and the epistemic power of gossip. *Ecological Thinking: The Politics of Epistemic Location* (2006) looks to ecological science as a place — literal and metaphorical — where knowledge is "naturally" made. Dr. Code is general editor of the *Routledge Encyclopedia of Feminist Theories* (2000) and of three feminist textbooks. Her current research addresses issues of vulnerability, incredulity, ignorance and trust.

Meg Luxton is a founding member of the School of Women's Studies and is a professor in Sociology, Social and Political Thought, and Women's Studies in the Faculty of Liberal and Professional Arts at York University. She has published widely on issues about women and work and is the co-editor of two recent collections: *Neo-Liberalism and Everyday Life* (with Susan Braedley, 2010) and *Social Reproduction: Feminist Political Economy Challenges Neo-Liberalism* (with Kate Bezanson, 2006). Dr. Luxton has acted as Director of the Graduate Program in Women's Studies and was the Director of the Centre for Feminist Research in 2009 when the U50 lectures were presented at York University.

Chandra Talpade Mohanty is Professor of Women's Studies and Dean's Professor of the Humanities at Syracuse University. Her work focuses on transnational feminist theory, studies of colonialism, imperialism and culture, and anti-racist education. Her scholarship focuses on the politics of difference and solidarity, the crossing of borders, the relation of feminist knowledges and scholarship to organizing and social movements, mobilizing a transnational feminist anti-capitalist critique, decolonizing knowledge, and theorizing agency, identity and resistance in the context of feminist solidarity. Dr. Mohanty's current work examines the politics of feminist anti-imperialist praxis in the academy and in social movements.

Mary Jane Mossman is Professor of Law at Osgoode Hall Law School at York University and was Director of Osgoode's Institute for Feminist Legal Studies 2002–2010, a co-sponsor of the U50 lectures that are included in this collection. Professor Mossman teaches and researches in family law and property law, and she is also regularly engaged in research about access to justice and the history of women in law. Professor Mossman's recent publications include "Comparing and Understanding Legal Aid Priorities" (with Karen Schucher and Claudia Schmeing, 2010) and *The First Women Lawyers: A Comparative Study of Gender, Law and the Legal Professions* (2006).

Janice Newson is Professor Emerita at York University, where she continues teaching in the Department of Sociology and its graduate program. Her scholarly work critiques the university's accommodation to corporatization, authoring (with Howard Buchbinder) *The University Means Business? Universities, Corporations and Academic Work* (1987); editing (with Jan Currie) *Universities and Globalisation: Critical Perspectives* (1998); and editing (with Claire Polster) *Academic Callings: The University We Have Had, Now Have, and Could Have* (2010). She has engaged in numerous activist projects challenging the corporatization of universities. Dr. Newson has also chaired the CAUT Status of Women Committee and been President of the Canadian Sociology and Anthropology Association.

Ann (Rusty) Shteir is a founding member of the School of Women's Studies, an early Director of the Graduate Program in Women's Studies, and Professor Emerita in Women's Studies and Humanities, Faculty of Liberal Arts and Professional Studies at York University. Her research interests are in the areas of women, gender, and science culture, eighteenth-century culture, feminist cultural history, natural history and the history of science writing. Her book, *Cultivating Science: Flora's Daughters and Botany in England, 1760 to 1860* (1996) received the Joan Kelly Memorial Prize for Women's History, American Historical Association, 1996. Dr. Shteir recently co-edited *Figuring It Out: Science, Gender, and Visual Culture* (2006), and her current project involves a study of representations of the goddess Flora in art, literature and science.

Margaret Thornton is an Australian Research Council Professorial Fellow at the College of Law, Australian National University in Canberra. She has also been a member of faculty at La Trobe and Macquarie Universities in Australia and a Visitor at a number of universities in Canada, the United States and the United Kingdom. Her recent work has focused on issues of feminism and the changing context for university teaching and research. Professor Thornton is the author of *The Liberal Promise* (human rights, 1990) and *Dissonance and Distrust* (women lawyers, 1997) and editor of several collections, the most recent of which is *Sex Discrimination in Uncertain Times* (2010).

Elisabeth Young-Bruehl was an American academic and psychoanalyst in Toronto and a member of the Toronto Psychoanalytic Society. She published a wide range of books, most notably award-winning biographies of Hannah Arendt and Anna Freud, but also including poetry and a novel. She edited a collection called *Freud on Women* (1992), and was a founding editor of the journal, *Studies in Gender and Sexuality*. Dr. Young-Bruehl's book, *The Anatomy of Prejudices* (1996), won the Association of American Publishers' prize for Best Book in Psychology in 1996, and her recent book on prejudice is called *Childism* (2011).

Introduction

PERSPECTIVES AND PASSIONS ABOUT FEMINISM AND THE ACADEMY

Mary Jane Mossman and Meg Luxton

> From its roots in a distinctive perception, feminist research is cre-
> ating a new knowledge... [and it] will help to create, in terms of
> philosophy, content, structure, a new education. Together, the new
> knowledge and the new education will change our views of society....
> With knowledge, and education, and time, we may, someday, create
> a new society. (Gow 1984: vii)

This confident prediction about the influence of feminist research formed
part of the introduction to a remarkable collection of academic presentations,
sponsored and then published in 1984 under the title, *Knowledge Reconsidered: A
Feminist Overview*, by the Canadian Research Institute for the Advancement of
Women (CRIAW) (Franklin et al. 1984). The papers reflected the focus of the
Seventh Annual CRIAW Conference, "Feminism in Action: New Knowledge,
New Education, New Society," a title that suggested considerable hopeful-
ness about the impact of feminist research on academic and social change
in Canada. The papers in the collection addressed these feminist aspirations from a number of different academic disciplines, including sociology
and anthropology, ethics, literary criticism, history and technological and
educational innovations. As the introduction to the publication explained,
the papers in *Knowledge Reconsidered: A Feminist Overview* were intended to
contribute to CRIAW's goal of "fostering a society in which women and men
are equal" (Gow 1984: x).

In 1981, just a few years prior to this CRIAW publication in Canada, a
similar essay collection appeared in the United States. Entitled *A Feminist
Perspective in the Academy: The Difference it Makes*, the editors (Elizabeth Langland
and Walter Gove) focused on the advent of women's studies programs and
their impressive effect on "the shape of what is known — and knowable —
in [academic] disciplines" (Langland and Gove 1981: 2). At the same time,
the editors noted that feminism had achieved less influence on university
curricula more generally. In this context, the editors argued forcefully that
feminism's focus on half of the human race means that it is not "an additional
knowledge merely to be tacked on to the curriculum [but] instead, a body

of knowledge that is *perspective transforming* and should therefore transform the existing curriculum from within and revise received notions of what constitutes an 'objective' or 'normative' perspective" (Langland and Gove 1981: 3–4, emphasis in original).

In the decades since these early feminist publications envisioned feminist research and teaching as creating new knowledge that is "perspective transforming," feminists in the academy have made significant contributions, both as knowers themselves and as contributors to the creation of knowledge. Their work has often been difficult and it has not always been successful. Moreover, while their efforts have sometimes been encouraged by developments outside the academy, they have also been inhibited or constrained by social, political and economic policies beyond academic boundaries. Feminists have also been both supported and resisted within the academy, as they have produced new scholarship, offered new disciplinary perspectives and disrupted many received notions. At the same time, feminist scholarship is nowhere near fully realizing the perspective transformation optimistically envisioned by the publications of the 1980s. Indeed, although this idea of transformation is familiar to feminists in the academy, it has proved to be remarkably elusive in practice.

Twenty-five years after the CRIAW publication, in 2009, feminist academics at York University created a lecture series, "Feminist Knowledge Reconsidered: Feminism and the Academy," specifically designed to revisit the ideas and themes addressed in feminist publications of the early 1980s, refocusing the lens on feminist knowledge in the academy. Jointly organized by York University's Centre for Feminist Research and Osgoode Hall Law School's Institute for Feminist Legal Studies, the lecture series was sponsored by York as part of its fiftieth anniversary celebrations. Six lectures were originally presented, some by feminist colleagues at York and others by visitors to the Centre and the Institute over a period of about fifteen months. Although the organizers of the lecture series selected the participants, each lecturer chose her individual topic to present to the York community — with all of the lectures intended to explore current ideas about feminism in relation to knowledge, education and society, and the future potential for feminist research and teaching in the university context.

The chapters in this collection represent revised versions of most of these special lectures, and they have been augmented by two additional chapters written by feminist colleagues at York. Together, they focus on a wide range of topics that reflect contemporary challenges for both feminism and the academy:

- the emergence of women's studies to become part of the academy, although (perhaps) without fundamentally "transforming" it;

- the ways in which complex theoretical and empirical connections can foster transformation in teaching and learning in the global academy for the future;
- the potential to use psychoanalytical insights to create knowledge that confronts underlying roots of prejudice and discrimination;
- the challenges for feminism as corporatization and technology increasingly (re)define the role of universities in a global world;
- the necessity to critique university responses to this new "knowledge" agenda and to foster research and teaching missions in the public interest;
- the need to (re)discover the history of women who challenged their exclusion from creating knowledge and art; and
- the importance of historical studies about the potential for feminist empiricism to subvert norms of objectivity in science and other forms of knowledge.

While all of the chapters reflect their authors' engagement with the title of the lecture series, each chapter also offers important insights about their individual research questions and how feminism has influenced their ways of posing them. Just as importantly, the chapters reveal how these feminist academics remain fully engaged with contemporary challenges for feminism in the academy, part of the ongoing project of knowledge (re)creation in a global world. As a collection, they invite readers to consider how feminist scholarship has transformed knowledge, how feminist scholarship in turn has been transformed and what feminist scholarship and teaching continue to offer to the academy and to our world.

As editors, our assessment of feminism in the academy differs in tone from the enthusiastic optimism expressed in *Knowledge Reconsidered: A Feminist Overview*. Our enthusiasm is more cautious, tempered by a concern to protect the gains of feminist scholarship and curricular developments in academic settings that are often deeply hostile to feminist goals and methods. And, as the chapters in this collection reveal, we need to employ both enthusiasm and caution strategically. As some of our Canadian feminist colleagues have suggested, it is "crucial to watch for… spaces and moments that are receptive to change, [because] social transformation is not simply a technical matter of devising exactly the right strategy to achieve equality" (Chunn, Boyd and Lessard 2007: 17). Thus, in seeking to characterize the current context, particularly by contrast with the 1984 CRIAW publication, we want to reflect briefly on the themes in the chapters in this collection, themes that reflect on ideas about change, including transformation (Bennett 2006; Coontz and Henderson 1986).

Feminism and the Academy: Revealing the "Other"

Although there are departments and programs in Canadian universities in the twenty-first century that focus on "women's studies" or "gender studies," the role of "feminism" in universities is more ambiguous.[1] As Luxton's chapter reveals, feminism in the academy was fostered initially by the ideas of the women's movement of the second half of the twentieth century and emerged from radical critiques of society among activists, some of whom were also academics. Although the precise nature of their critiques differed, feminist academics challenged and changed the landscape of universities in the 1970s and 1980s, not only in relation to ideas about gendered knowledge in their research and teaching, but also with respect to institutional politics and policies. In addition, feminist academic initiatives based on de Beauvoir's idea of the "Other" opened up intellectual spaces in the academy for new areas of study in relation to those who had been traditionally excluded from academic knowledge, including programs about Indigenous peoples, Black studies, antiracist initiatives, sexuality programs, dis/ability research and peace and social justice studies. In this context, feminists who were collaborating across disciplines recognized the need for an interdisciplinary approach to studying women. Luxton argues in her chapter:

> The core questions that animated much early feminist scholarship were: how to explain the origins and persistence of men's dominance and women's subordination across many different societies, through so many historical periods, and despite the diversity of women in any given society or period, based on a range of hierarchical social relations such as class, national origin, race and ethnicity, age, ability and sexual orientation; and how to inform and inspire struggles for greater equality or liberation.

Moreover, Luxton argues that these questions remain critical for contemporary feminist scholars and students, not only in Canada but in other parts of the world — everywhere that women's equality remains a goal not yet fully realized.

In this context, the chapter by Alexander and Mohanty revisits some of Luxton's themes about current challenges for feminism in the academy. For these authors, the production of feminist knowledge requires (re)connection and collaboration between the academy and feminist activism; and moreover, new cartographies in research and teaching must also mobilize knowledge about the transnational:

> Can transnational feminist lenses push us to ask questions that are location specific but not necessarily location bound? If we take seriously the mandate to do collaborative work in and outside the

academy, the kind of work that would demystify the borders between inside and outside and thereby render them porous rather than mythically fixed, it is imperative that the academy *not* be the only location that determines our research and pedagogical work; that we recognize those hierarchies of place within the multiple sites and locations in which knowledge is produced, and we maintain clarity about the origin of the production of knowledge and the spaces where this knowledge travels.

In their chapter, the authors examine thirteen core university syllabi from women's and gender studies programs, and from LGBTT/queer studies programs, in a variety of colleges and universities in the United States to assess the relationship between the politics of location and the politics of knowledge production and who is able to make "sustainable claims" about these links. Such questions clearly make the feminist project in the academy an integral part of a revised liberation agenda for the whole social world, including Canada and the United States.

Young-Bruehl's chapter documents how some kinds of liberation have occurred with respect to issues of sexuality, thus confronting the prejudice and discrimination that has so often accompanied difference. According to Young-Bruehl, it was the combined effect of the women's liberation movement and the gay liberation movement that resulted in the recognition (and acceptance, at least to some extent) of sexual diversity: "in the domain of scientific study of sex, the result of the political shift and the paradigm shift has been that the biological sex binary male and female has become a continuum that includes all kinds of intersex states between the extremes of male and female." Her paper provides a brief overview of historical and recent developments in the scientific study of sex, suggesting that current practices of tolerance for sexual diversity reflect sexuality as "a manifestation of a bodyspirit harmony… and [that] how this harmony is manifested is a matter of choice or practice." In addition, Young-Bruehl argues that sexual pathology is now viewed scientifically in terms of abuse, rather than deviancy: that is, "the focus is now on the quality of the relationship existing between persons engaging in sexual behaviours." In this context, she suggests that the focus now should be on those who engage in abusive sexual behaviours, particularly against children. As her paper clearly demonstrates, some intellectual ideas (even those related to scientific knowledge) may change.

Feminism and the Academy:
(Re)Engaging the "Knowledge Revolution"

Although all the chapters focus, at least to some extent, on challenges for feminism in the contemporary academy, Thornton's chapter provides a detailed analysis of aspects of the "knowledge revolution" that is occurring in the academy in many different parts of the world. As she argues, universities, once regarded as "the custodian of culture, the seat of higher learning and the paradigmatic site of free inquiry," have been turned upside down, so that "the university as a key knowledge producer is now primarily regarded as a source of wealth creation to be exploited." Thus, although feminist critiques of knowledge achieved some success in the academy in the late twentieth century, Thornton argues that the impact of neoliberalism, the new knowledge economy (in which know-how is valued over know-what) and globalization have shifted university goals from civil society to the market. Thus, in the context of new goals of profitability and "technopreneurial" projects, the role of critique (including feminist critique) is largely seen as dispensable, and "the legitimation of inequality tilts the scales permanently in favour of the status quo." While recognizing the formidable challenges for feminists in the academy, Thornton nonetheless suggests that there is an urgent need for feminist and progressive scholars to continue to exercise the roles of "critic and conscience" in this new knowledge economy, rather than being mere pawns in its promotion.

In her chapter focused more specifically on developments in Canadian universities in the past twenty-five years, Newson reviews three different stages in higher education policies, suggesting that these developments have substantially undermined the role of universities as institutions serving the public interest. Her focus on the processes of policy-making within the academy, and especially collective responses by academic communities to governmental initiatives, unmasks the ways in which members of the academy have often embraced changes that are transforming/undermining its role as an institution for the public good. Significantly, Newson suggests that these changes reflect a two-way process, in which economic and political influences (once considered external to program development within universities) move into the academic domain; at the same time, however, there is also an energetic movement outward on the part of universities to sell their services to specific clienteles and customers. "In this, the university has been an agent in its own right." Like Thornton, Newson identifies some of the results of these changes, including a loss of public trust in universities, the skewing of research proposals and methodologies, the rise of student consumerism and the pressure to demonstrate regular productivity (which may limit large-scale, time-consuming and important research). Like Thornton, Newson also argues for feminists and other progressive scholars to continue to offer a radical critique, in spite of these challenges, quoting John Ralston Saul's insight:

We know that universities are in crisis and are attempting to ride out the storm by aligning themselves with various corporate interests. That is short-sighted and self destructive. *From the point of view of their obligation to society, it is simply irresponsible.* (Saul 1995: 173, emphasis in Newson)

Feminism and the Academy:
Remembering History/Recalling Resistance

All of the chapters in this collection reflect their authors' commitment to the creation of feminist knowledge and to continuing resistance to efforts to negate its radical critique, both within and outside the academy. Perhaps because of the strength of current opposition, most of the chapters focus on current and future challenges. Yet, we must also remember how women throughout history have also adopted many different strategies to overcome their exclusion from knowing and learning and to become the creators of knowledge themselves. Two chapters in this collection serve to remind us particularly of the history of feminist knowledge.

Shteir's chapter focuses on a group of women in England in the eighteenth century, known as "Bluestockings," who met regularly for literary and intellectual conversation and to cultivate and promote the ideals of the Enlightenment. In a context in which women were often excluded from universities (and from learning), such women nonetheless chose to pursue a life of the mind, as learned women, professional artists and active published writers, although "it was not easy" to do so. Yet, as Shteir's chapter reveals, Elizabeth Carter (1717–1806) succeeded as a classical scholar, poet and translator, and her publications included treatises and philosophical work translated from French, Italian and Greek. Similarly, Angelica Kauffman (1741–1807) lived as a young woman painter in Italy and then moved to England and became an established painter there as well as a founding member of the Royal Academy. In addition to demonstrating the achievements of these women, Shteir also demonstrates the significance of cultural interpretations of the paintings (and self-portraits) of these learned women, often portrayed as the goddesses Minerva and Flora. For Shteir, feminist knowledge requires us to "take the past more seriously" in order to find new strategies and opportunities:

> It is highly likely... that in most times and places we can find examples of how an individual woman or group of women negotiated, positioned herself, resisted, failed to thrive, pushed at boundaries, subverted and critiqued. Feminist cultural history will be enriched by looking, looking more and looking again, at groups and individuals in the past... we are not the first or second generation of feminist scholars that is seeking to shape knowledge that will change the

world. Scholarship is feminist activism too, and we should be making it work for us.

By contrast with Shteir's chapter about eighteenth century women, Code's chapter tells the story of Rachel Carson, a mid-twentieth century woman whose scientific practices unsettled epistemological orthodoxy by suggesting a need to take account of sites and locations in creating scientific knowledge, an argument that forcefully challenged ideas about knowledge as both objective and universal:

> Translated into the realm of knowledge-seeking processes… the implication is that where, when, how and by whom knowledge is made and circulated may need to be investigated in evaluating the knowledge itself: that it is implausible and indeed careless to assume without question that knowledge transcends the circumstances of its making, to claim universal pertinence.

In the context of her scientific research, Carson's reliance on experience and contextual situation significantly diminished acceptance of her findings, primarily because of the lowly status of experience in positivist-empiricist knowledge projects. Code's description of the rejection of findings in later research projects, similarly based on experiential evidence, reveals how positivism remains firmly in place in the current knowledge economy. For Code, Carson's (subversive) work suggests that feminist epistemology in the twenty-first century, "in its engagement with particularity, diversity and the multiplicity of situation and circumstance within and among women, can no longer be conceived… as a self-contained inquiry, distinct from ethical, political and other feminist projects." Moreover, as Code suggested in her earlier work, the impact of feminism on epistemology is to move the question "Whose knowledge are we talking about?" to a central place (Code 1989).

Concluding Comments

The chapters in this collection reflect the scholarly preoccupations and passions of feminist academics in a variety of academic disciplines and contexts. They are intended to reveal some of the current dilemmas and controversies for feminism in the academy and in the creation of knowledge. Some are more hopeful than others about the future of feminism within the academy, some are engaged in redesigning the feminist academic project to create new kinds of knowledge, and some focus their energies on resisting hostile or negative challenges both inside the academy and beyond. All the chapters agree, however, that feminism has made important contributions to knowledge and that feminist scholars and students need to continue this work, however difficult it may sometimes appear.

What is clear is that feminism has not gone away at York University, in Canada, or elsewhere — it is still a presence in the academy, feminists are still among those who are knowers and feminism is still contributing to knowledge in our universities and in our society. For us, the editors of this collection, while we agree that the optimism of the 1984 CRIAW essays may no longer be quite as appropriate in the twenty-first century academy, we nonetheless believe that feminism's continuing contribution to knowledge remains significant, even fundamental, to the future transformation of knowledge in the academy and in our world.

Note

1.   At York University, there is a Centre for Feminist Research and Osgoode Hall's Institute for Feminist Legal Studies, both created in the late 1980s/early 1990s, which foster research, support visitors and provide interdisciplinary programs and seminars.However, academic programs for students are generally offered by the School of Women's Studies, recently renamed the School of Gender, Sexuality and Women's Studies. Clearly, names matter, as was evident in the furor about women's studies programs in Canada in early 2010. More significantly, some universities have recently been dismantling these programs (Luxton, this volume)

References

Bennett, Judith. 2006. *History Matters: Patriarchy and the Challenge of Feminism*. Philadelphia: University of Pennsylvania Press.

Chunn, Dorothy, Susan Boyd, and Hester Lessard. 2007. "Feminism, Law, and Social Change: An Overview." In Chunn, Boyd and Lessard (eds.), *Reaction and Resistance: Feminism, Law, and Social Change*. Vancouver: UBC Press.

Code, Lorraine. 1989. "The Impact of Feminism on Epistemology." In Nancy Tuana (ed.), *American Philosophical Association Newsletter* on Feminism and Philosophy 88.2 (Winter): 25–29.

Coontz, Stephanie, and Pete Henderson. 1986. "Introduction: 'Explanations' of Male Dominance." In Coontz and Henderson (eds.), *Women's Work, Men's Property: The Origins of Gender and Class*. London: Verso.

Franklin, Ursula, Michèle Jean, Sylvia Van Kirk, Andrea Lebowitz, Meg Luxton, Susan Sherwin, and Dorothy E. Smith. 1984. *Knowledge Reconsidered: A Feminist Overview*. Ottawa: CRIAW.

Gow, June. 1984. "Preface." In Ursula Franklin, Michèle Jean, Sylvia Van Kirk, Andrea Lebowitz, Meg Luxton, Susan Sherwin, and Dorothy E. Smith (eds,). *Knowledge Reconsidered: A Feminist Overview*. Ottawa: CRIAW.

Langland, Elizabeth, and Walter Gove (eds.). 1981. "Editors' Notes." In *A Feminist Perspective in the Academy: The Difference it Makes*. Chicago and London: University of Chicago Press.

Saul, John Ralston. 1995. *The Unconscious Civilization: The 1995 Massey Lectures*. Toronto: Anansi Press.

Part One

FEMINISM AND THE ACADEMY: REVEALING THE "OTHER"

Chapter One

FEMINISM AND THE ACADEMY
Transforming Knowledge?

Meg Luxton

Feminist Challenges, Challenging Feminism

From its inception, feminist scholarship has faced criticism that it has little or no scholarly legitimacy because it is linked to a political project. In January 2010, for example, a national newspaper in Canada denounced women's studies as "these angry, divisive and dubious programs" (*National Post* 2010: A12). The year before, in the U.S., the courts ruled on a case brought by a lawyer against Columbia University, arguing that, in offering women's studies, Columbia was biased against men (Kilgannon 2009). Few other academic disciplines face comparable attacks and denunciations. Business schools that promote free enterprise, capitalist profit-making are honoured; philosophy departments that teach the value of classical Greek scholars without critiquing their sexism and elitism are revered. Both reflect explicit political projects. So why is feminist scholarship singled out for such vitriolic attack and subjected to such ongoing scrutiny?

Feminist scholarship traces its English language roots to the women and men of late eighteenth century Britain and Europe, who protested against women's subordination and denounced women's exclusion from the institutions of political and economic power. They demanded access to education as one central route to greater economic, social and political power and to greater equality with men at the same time as they questioned some of the great truths of European formal knowledge[1] and argued for new ways of knowing (Rowbotham 1972; see Chapter Six volume). At its core, contemporary English-language feminist scholarship, like its antecedents, is based on four related initiatives: revealing the dynamics of women's subordination, with the goal of reducing or eliminating it; exposing the sexism that is fundamental to prevailing formal knowledge systems; generating new knowledge that takes account of gender relations; and fighting for women's access to education and the economic, social and political arenas available to educated men. Feminism is also closely linked to other critiques of the status quo, particularly those which reveal the deep-rooted biases that have historically privileged and legitimated elite, white, heterosexual, Euro-North

American men; its existence threatens this ongoing privilege and undermines its legitimacy (Rowbotham 1972). Thus, many of those who benefit from the current system have vested interests in denying the validity of feminist analyses and opposing the claims of feminist politics; indeed, the intensity of their hostility is one measure of feminism's success.

In this chapter, I argue that by the early twenty-first century, while feminist scholarship has a well-established legitimacy in the systems of formal knowledge production, it remains vulnerable, subject on the one hand to anti-feminist mobilizations (Dubinsky 1985) and, on the other, to claims that feminism is redundant because women's subordination no longer exists (Hawkesworth 2004). Perhaps even more insidiously, women's issues are often subsumed under equity issues, an apparently benign initiative that easily erodes the focus on women.[2]

Concentrating on Canada since the mid-twentieth century, this chapter begins by showing how, as women finally entered universities in significant numbers, English-language feminist scholarship challenged the established systems of formal knowledge and gained a foothold in the academy. But in doing so, feminist scholarship itself was challenged and forced to change, often in ways that contradicted its initial aspirations. I illustrate the dynamics of those challenges by considering the creation by feminist scholarship of a new (interdisciplinary) discipline, women's studies. This chapter then explores some of the current tensions and dilemmas facing feminist scholarship and concludes by insisting that the feminist political project remains vital and that feminist scholarship remains fundamental to its success.

Feminist Challenges to the Systems of Formal Knowledge Production

In 1952 Simone de Beauvoir revealed that the "representation of the world, like the world itself, is the work of men; they describe it from their own point of view, which they confuse with absolute truth" (de Beauvoir 1972: 161). For example her colleague, Claude Levi-Strauss, a leading anthropologist, in writing about his field work among the Bororo people of the Brazilian Amazon, illustrates the kind of representation of the world she was critiquing: "*Le village entier partit le lendemain dans une trentaine de pirogues, nous laissant seuls avec les femmes et les enfants dans les maisons abandonnées*" [The entire village left the next day in about thirty canoes, leaving us alone with the women and children in the abandoned houses] (Levi-Strauss 1936: 283).

Simone de Beauvoir's scathing assessment of the sexism intrinsic to the formal knowledge systems of Europe and North America laid the basis for the challenges to formal knowledge raised in the next few decades by scholars and activists. In the late 1960s, part of a widespread radicalization around the world, the women's liberation movement and a revitalised women's equality movement mobilized thousands of women and men who enthusiastically assumed women could and should challenge all areas of men's privilege (Andersen 2010).

The movement of women into universities and colleges in Canada as in most English-speaking regions was one such challenge. Fuelled by the expansion of universities and colleges, the gradual hiring of women faculty and the dramatic influx of women students, there was, for the first time in history, a critical mass of women legitimately integrated into the systems of formal knowledge production. Their very presence disrupted centuries of men's privilege but, more significantly, many of the new generation of scholars were deeply influenced by the radical politics of the period and mobilized to challenge the traditional practices of the universities. The academic wing of that women's movement levelled a range of criticisms at the academy: its structures, personnel and culture were all masculine and excluded women; and the curriculum was profoundly androcentric, ignoring women most of the time, glossing the experiences of (often elite, white) men as representative of all human life in the profoundly ambiguous notion of Man (Lloyd 1984). It was often deeply sexist or misogynist, reflecting entrenched beliefs that legitimated women's oppression with claims of biological and historical inevitability. The prevailing theories of the human sciences in that period assumed that men and women were significantly different biologically and socially, and that any efforts to challenge or interfere with such sex differences were both naïvely unrealisable and inappropriately socially disruptive (Luxton 1984).

Feminist scholarship as a field of study in Canada emerged in the 1960s, engendered on the one hand by frustration and anger when women's critiques of the academy were ignored or denied, and on the other by new passions and excitement as women scholars developed new "ways of seeing" women and gender relations (Jean 1984) and created new ways of learning and knowing (*Atlantis* 1990: XVI, 1). Feminist scholarship in academia developed in two related ways. In penetrating existing disciplines, it created discipline-based studies of women and gender, and new critiques about the ways in which the disciplines were deformed by their failure to include women and gender relations. One result was a flourishing of studies of women: women's history, a sociology of women, women and the law, women and science, woman and dance or the study of literature by, for and about women. Another result was a reworking of academic disciplines to take women and gender seriously in both teaching and scholarship and to challenge the established canons in the various fields (Armstrong and Hamilton 1985).

At the same time, feminist scholars argued that no single dimension, whether biological, sexual, cultural, economic, legal, psychological, political or historicist, is adequate to explain the origins and persistence of gender hierarchies or to offer guidelines for women's struggles for equality or liberation.

They argued for an understanding of women's situation as a multidimensional complex of material and ideological forces, fundamentally structured by power relations, and importantly understood across international, transnational and comparative dimensions. As a result, feminist scholarship, and especially feminist theory, developed as resolutely interdisciplinary and with a strong transnational orientation (Maroney and Luxton 1987).

In its early period in the 1960s and 1970s, feminist academics had a close relationship to the larger women's movement. Some faculty came to feminist scholarship with a primary orientation to the academy, inspired by their research and personal experiences to take up feminist issues. Others came from the radical activist women's liberation movement and, at least initially, understood their scholarship and engagement with the university as activist politics, an orientation that was shared with many students and some staff. The main issues of the women's movement became topics of research and the books written by feminist academics influenced the political actions of the women's movement (Cohen et al. 1993; Cohen and Pierson 1995). Movement activists were invited guest speakers in classes and academic feminists contributed their expertise to the service of women's organizing. The debates and controversies shaping feminist scholarship informed and reflected the politics of the larger political struggles of the period (Adamson, Briskin and McPhail 1989; Rebick 2005).

Two of the main political struggles that deeply influenced feminist scholarship, and particularly the development of feminist theory, related to different understandings of systemic inequalities and how they might be reduced or eliminated. One was between the positions advocated by Marxists, socialists and other left wing radicals critical of dominant bourgeois or liberal democracy and the capitalist economic system who called for its overthrow, and those who called for its reform (Geutell 1974; Jagger and Rosenberg 1978). The other involves efforts to transform the English-language feminism that developed in Europe and North America into a transnational movement that more genuinely recognises the diversity of issues confronting women around the world (Mohanty 2003). Both struggles shaped the women's movement and feminist scholarship and profoundly affected the interventions feminism made in the academy.

As feminist scholarship in universities grew in the late 1970s and matured through the 1980s into the 1990s, it changed the landscape of academia. Because feminism is both an intellectual project and a political movement, feminist academics were inevitably centrally involved in transforming knowledge production and engaged in the institutional politics concerned with not only what kind of knowledge is produced, but how it is produced (Briskin 2002). Feminist academics opened up new areas of research and generated new curriculum (see Chapters Two and Seven); they transformed teaching and learning practices (Briskin 1990; Parry 1996). One of its most important acquisitions was captured by the concept of "intersectionality." Initially coined by Kimberle Crenshaw (1989), intersectionality recognizes that the different systems of domination and oppression — such as those based on sex and gender, class, race and ethnicity, nationality, religion, sexual orientation, disability or age — interrelate, creating complex systems that reflect the intersection of the multiple forms of oppression and domination. This understanding anchored the efforts to make feminist scholarship transnational and to reflect of the diversity of women.

Such efforts stimulated universities to establish programs of study focused on others excluded from the traditional curriculum: gender and sexuality studies, Aboriginal and Indigenous studies, Black studies, anti-racist studies, and peace and social justice studies (see Chapter Three; MacDonald 1998; Bondy 2010: 4). Feminists also worked to open faculty spaces to people who had previously been excluded: lesbians, gay men, trans people, people of colour and Aboriginal peoples. In taking seriously the slogan, "the personal is political," feminism challenged students and faculty to examine their own lives, exploring the contradictions of their desires and fears, and struggling for a self-understanding that recognizes both forces shaping one's life and opportunities to grow and change into future selves (Rowbotham 1973; Segal 1999). Such changes were hard won, requiring their advocates to fight long-standing traditions and practices (Eichler 1985).

Just sixty years after *The Second Sex* was published in English, feminist scholarship has so transformed representations of the world that Simone de Beauvoir's claims no longer resonate. Feminist scholarship now offers representations of the world by women as well as men, from a wide range of differing perspectives. Feminist scholarship has revealed the fundamental significance of women's (often unpaid) work to the world and it has discredited any notion of an absolute truth. Feminist scholarship exists in many academic disciplines and is a recognized sub-field in most. Feminist research and writing is widely available in many languages and reflects the perspectives of peoples from many parts of the world. Women's studies programs exist in many countries and a growing number of undergraduate students are now taught by faculty who have attained all their degrees in women's studies. Yet, in spite of these successes, feminist scholarship remains vulnerable, and feminist challenges to formal knowledge systems remain defiant rather than firmly established. Too many scholars continue to do research and writing that ignores women and the extensive contributions of feminist scholarship, arguing, if challenged, that feminist scholarship is being done elsewhere or that the concerns of feminism are no longer relevant (if they ever were) (Hutchison 2010: 1).

The Systems of Formal Knowledge Production Challenge Feminism

The ways in which each discipline engaged with feminist interventions varied enormously, reflecting the subject matter, and the ways in which women practitioners had been incorporated historically (Paludi and Steuernagel 1990). Disciplines that dealt directly with human social relations, such as the humanities, social sciences, the professions and applied sciences, tended to be the first to face feminist challenges. Some, such as anthropology, sociology, history, literature and social work tolerated feminist scholarship early on (Luxton 1984; Lerner 1997). Others such as geography, psychology, philosophy, political science, economics and medicine were more resistant. The natural and formal sciences were less vulnerable to challenges to their core knowledge bases but faced charges of systemic discrimination by woman seeking access. The academic professions and applied sciences were also shaped by the position of women in professional practices outside the university, as, for example, social workers, medical practitioners or lawyers.

The way feminism was integrated into or resisted by a particular discipline also depended on a variety of contingent factors: the disciplinary traditions of a particular country and language[3], the role of a particular scholar, the support in a particular department or school or the particular orientation of the key gatekeepers of the discipline (Eichler 1981). Typically, feminist interventions in the existing disciplines included both intellectual reworkings and political revampings. Feminists accumulated knowledge about women and gender relations and insisted that such knowledge be taken up seriously in the discipline. They developed critiques of the ways in which androcentrism had distorted existing knowledge; they reworked existing theoretical models, methodologies and research methods to take account of feminism; and they monitored efforts to include women practioners in all aspects of the profession. At the same time, they drew on feminist scholarship in other disciplines for conceptual inspiration and empirical data while collaborating with other feminists to support the integration of feminist scholarship into academia. In doing so, they produced new interdisciplinary knowledge, methodologies and feminist theory. The combined result over the past thirty years has been a burgeoning and massive body of feminist scholarship (Robbins, Luxton, Eichler and Descarriers 2008).

Academic feminists mobilized different strategies to anchor their scholarship. Some were committed to their disciplines and found their discipline amenable to their research and teaching. They worried that forming separate programs could ghettoize feminist scholarship and leave unchallenged existing disciplinary practices. They focussed on transforming the existing disciplines to include feminism and to expand disciplinary boundaries to accommodate interdisciplinary perspectives. Others, in creating explicitly new interdisciplinary studies, crafted women's studies as a new field of study, initially as individual courses, then as degree-granting programs and university departments, with the related professional infrastructure of academic journals, professional associations and conferences.

There is now an extensive literature documenting feminist interventions into the disciplines and smaller body of work exploring the development of women's studies, especially in the United States (for Canada, see Braithwaite et al. 2004; Crow and Guetell 2007; Robbins, Luxton, Eichler and Descarriers 2008; for the U.S., see Boxer 1998; O'Barr 1994; Lerner 1997; Winkler and DiPalma 1999). Here I consider women's studies, based on experiences in English-language universities in Canada, asking what shaped its development, what challenges it faces in the current period, and how it has contributed to new forms of knowledge production and professional practices and to sustaining feminist politics inside and out side the academy.

Women's Studies: An Interdisciplinary "Discipline"

The impulse to set up women's studies as autonomous programs, which eventually produced a distinct interdisciplinary "discipline", came primarily from the core questions that animated much early feminist scholarship: how to explain the origins and persistence of men's dominance and women's subordination across many different societies, through so many changing historical periods, and despite the diversity of women in any given society or period, based on a range of hierarchical social relations such as class, national origin, race and ethnicity, age, ability, and sexual orientation; and how to inform and inspire struggles for greater equality or liberation. The early recognition that no single dimension can offer an adequate analysis necessitated and inspired interdisciplinarity.

The logic of interdisciplinarity produced a body of feminist theory and methodology which is informed by contributions from many disciplines but has emerged as a distinctive field in itself — the intellectual justification for recognising women's studies as a distinct discipline.

The argument for separate women's studies courses and degree programs was strengthened both when faculty collaboration across disciplines generated interest in the academic equivalent of "a room of their own"[4] and when opposition to feminist scholarship in specific departments drove faculty and students to seek alternative locations. Efforts to set up interdisciplinary women's studies courses and degree-granting programs were complicated by the relative inflexibility of most university discipline-based administrative structures[5]. The ability to hire women's studies professors was hampered by regulations that required faculty to be appointed to a discipline-based department, while attempts to set up women's studies departments (which could hire) were thwarted by the lack of available faculty. Few universities could easily accommodate programs that attempted to integrate units that were housed in separate faculties (such as Humanities and Social Sciences, Law and Health Sciences), generating endless complications about everything from budget-lines to course credits. These efforts were further complicated by the financial constraints most universities faced throughout the period. As a consequence, those attempting to establish women's studies in the universities had to spend inordinate amounts of time and effort "bucking the system." Most women's studies advocates point out that their programs were built by the volunteer labour of dedicated faculty, staff and students (Eichler 1985).

Women's studies programs have faced struggles that rarely troubled other disciplines. Women's studies programs present themselves as innova-tive, pedagogically progressive and committed to fighting oppression and inequality. And so they are constantly under pressure, especially from their students, to live up to that promise. The dilemma this poses is that the most underfunded, weak and vulnerable units in the university are expected to provide leadership and allocate resources in the fight against the systemic discrimination that pervades the institution as a whole. Women's studies pro-grams are criticized for not hiring women of colour or Aboriginal women, for not offering enough courses on working class or lesbian and trans lives, in ways that political science and engineering programs rarely are.

Intellectually, interdisciplinarity posed serious challenges too. To be genuinely effective, interdisciplinarity demands of its practitioners a thorough knowledge of multiple disciplines before efforts to combine, integrate and move beyond them are possible. Until 1997 when the first PhD in women's studies graduated, all women's studies faculty came from other disciplines. They not only had to remain versed in their discipline of origin but had to take on a range of new ways of knowing which feminist scholarship was employing to develop its new theory and research. Any sophisticated interdisciplinary research requires an unusual breadth and depth of its practitioners. It is all too easy for students and scholars to draw on superficial understandings of various traditions, mobilizing theoretical concepts whose implications they only partially understand. Too often, the result is "an amiable but sloppy eclecticism which attempts to patch together traditions based on divergent paradigms" (Maroney and Luxton 1984: 3).

As feminist scholarship was institutionalised in autonomous programs or departments, it was typically called "women's studies." Many of its ad-vocates argued for "feminist studies," but the counter arguments, positively, that students might be put off and negatively, that feminist studies was too overtly political, carried the day. Women's studies has the advantage of fo-cusing on women and conforms to the general pattern of interdisciplinary area studies (Canadian studies, labour studies, Indigenous studies, health studies). However, as feminist scholarship has grown and expanded, many have complained that the name "women's studies" is constraining and fails to recognize the actual work going on under its rubric: gender, queer, sexuality, disability and critical race studies.

Some institutions have changed the name of their program to be more explicitly inclusive: Queens' University offers Gender Studies, Simon Fraser University and York University offer Gender, Sexuality and Women's Studies, Nipissing University has a Gender Equality and Social Justice Department. But some worry that changing the name feeds the political claim that feminism is either no longer relevant or is discriminatory and could undermine the importance of a focus on women and their on-going oppression. They wonder if the initiative to move to gender or equity studies is a perverse outcome of the commitment to an intersectional approach. They point out that it is possible to offer gender studies without ever discussing women, much less acknowledging women's continued oppression and there is no guarantee that equity studies, women's issues will remain at the forefront.

As many undergraduate women's studies programs continue to be underfunded and short staffed, they struggle to get by, relying on faculty and staff who put in hours of unpaid and unrecognized service, and they are constantly under pressure to justify their existence in institutions where the financial bottom line increasingly drives the agenda (see Chapters Four and Five). In April 2009 the University of Guelph eliminated its Women's Studies program, despite widespread protests, on campus, across Canada and internationally. Caught in a double bind for years, the program was chronically underfunded which kept enrolments low and, as a result, it was unable to attract enough students to warrant more funding. According to former coordinator Professor Helen Hoy, the administration employed two arguments to justify closing the program. It claimed that it could not afford to keep the program open given the university's fiscal crisis, even though the closure saved only 0.17 percent of the university's budget shortfall. Hoy said the administration also suggested that women's studies was "out-dated and at an impasse" and considered changing to a Sex, Sexuality and Gender Studies program, a name that "would sound less parochial or restrictive or [less] unpalatable for those who aren't prepared to initially consider themselves feminist" (Bondy 2010). Guelph students protested Women's Studies' demise with a funeral and headstone inscribed "RIP Feminism: Apparently We Don't Need You" (Bondy 2010). Media coverage of this closure prompted the vitriolic attack on women's studies programs in Canada that referred to them as "angry, divisive and dubious programs" (*National Post* 2010: A12).

By 2010, women's studies undergraduate programs were well-established in most universities and a number also offered graduate degrees. There were twelve PhD programs in women's studies and/or gender studies and about sixty graduates with PhDs in women's studies.[6] It is unclear to what extent the Guelph experience may prefigure an erosion of free-standing women's studies programs. What is clear is that the research being produced by the first generation of women's studies graduates is affirming the place of inter-disciplinary feminism in the legions of formal knowledge production.

Feminism, Scholarship and Formal Knowledge in Movement

In the more than forty years since feminist scholarship established a base in the universities, both its intellectual and its political projects have changed significantly. There have been some important gains; at the same time, some of the troubling issues facing contemporary feminists might look familiar to their predecessors. Women students in Canada attend university in almost the same numbers as men. By 2008, women were just over half of BA and MA students and just under half of PhD students (CAUT 2010: 21). The proportion of women faculty members has increased to 34 percent, up from 29 percent in 2001 (CAUT 2010: 6). Women have gained access to the universities.

But after repeated evidence that the prestigious and well-funded (by the federal government) Canada Research Chairs were being given dispropor-tionately to white men, a team of eight women made a formal complaint, alleging discrimination, before the Canadian Human Rights Commission. It was settled in 2006 by a negotiated agreement but, despite that, women remain underrepresented. No data are reported for other equity groups — Aboriginal peoples, racialized minorities and persons with disabilities — despite their inclusion in the settlement agreement (Side and Robbins 2007). In the 2010 competition for the first nineteen Canada Excellence Research Chairs, even more prestigious and well-funded research positions, not one woman was appointed and no women were included in the short list of thirty-six proposals (Church 2010: 1; Robbins 2010).

These patterns are part of a much larger pattern of growing inequality in Canada. Between 1997 and 2007 the richest 1 percent of Canadians in-creased their wealth while the standard of living of the majority of Canadians declined (Yalnizyan 2010). Universities are not immune to such trends and, as tuition fees increase, university elitism is strengthened. The struggles to reduce economic, social and political inequality remain.

Feminism established itself as an increasingly legitimate area of study and developed an institutional presence in a period when the broader rad-ical women's movement lost some of its momentum (Nguyen 2010). The flourishing of scholarship and its penetration into most areas of intellectual endeavour means much of it explores a range of topics only indirectly related to the explicit political project. As feminist scholarship developed, its prac-titioners were increasingly drawn from the academy, not from the women's movement, and while many of them were sympathetic to community-based activism, few had any experience of direct involvement. Increasingly, feminist academics learned their feminism in classrooms rather than in the women's movement. At the same time, feminist scholars were pulled toward each other by their shared critique of sexism, their mutual efforts to improve women's situations in the universities and their excitement in building feminist scholarship. This built stronger ties among feminist scholars and was important in securing a place for feminism in the universities. But those efforts to build a broader feminist scholarship easily undermined the radical edge of women's liberation scholarship, as liberation politics were dropped in the interests of building an inclusive women's studies.

Concurrently, the activist women's movement lost its place on the public political agenda. For example, after its election in 2006, feminism came under explicit attack by Conservative Prime Minister Stephen Harper and his minority government (Dobbin 2010). Status of Women Canada was told to remove women's equality from its mandate in September 2006 (although they reinstated it quietly later) (Clancy 2006). Women's services were forced to abandon advocacy to retain access to government funding, twelve out of sixteen Status of Women's offices throughout Canada were closed, the Courts Challenges Program was eliminated and a funding agreement on universal child care abandoned (Brennan 2010). In that climate, many junior faculty and students were dubious about feminism, seeing it as outdated or negative, something they did not want to associate with. As its opponents celebrated the demise of feminism, and some of its apparent allies claimed to have achieved post-feminism, debates emerged within feminist scholarship about the extent to which feminist scholarship had lost its radical edge and, if it had, the extent to which that is a problem (Scott 2008). There is a wealth of knowledge about women's subordination, about gender relations and about efforts to challenge sexism but the direct link between feminist scholarship and the women's movement has weakened.

This uncoupling was reinforced by the real politik of academic life for most feminists. As academic feminists fought to establish their scholarship in the disciplines and women's studies programs, their activism focused on the university. To demanding teaching and research workloads, feminists added administrative and service work, heavy demands that made it difficult for faculty to be involved in activism outside the university. At one level this is a practical question: lecturing one day and picketing the next leave most faculty exhausted. But at another level, it is a more challenging question about the relationship of the university and formal knowledge production to the world of which it is a part. It is the question about the role of the intellectual in society,

In the late twentieth century and early twenty-first century, the Anglo-American world typically repressed discussion about this question and the dominant culture is dismissive of those deemed to be intellectuals (Gramsci 2001; Showalter 2000).[7]One outcome in the women's movement was that distinctions were made between those who were primarily involved in, and committed to, on the one hand, the practical, and on the other, the intellectual (McRobbie 1982: 8). As Angela McRobbie (1982: 8) notes,

> women whose work involves periods of intense privatised labour, like writing, paining or reading, are seen as less committed than those who spend the entire working day and often more, working with other women — battered women, delinquent girls, schoolgirls or isolated housewives.

Feminists working in women's crisis centres are understood in the women's movement to be activists doing front-line activist work. But those who focus on university politics or who concentrate on their intellectual work as researchers, writers and teachers are typically seen as advancing their own careers. Those teaching feminism to hundreds of students each week typically are not recognized by others as activists. It is a painful irony when those same professors are accused by anti-feminists of being "too political" and not conforming to objective standards of scholarship.

However, as the numbers of women's groups and popular publications have decreased, women's studies is one of the few accessible institutional spaces for feminism, one of the easiest places for people to get information about and become politically involved in the women's movement. Despite the ongoing troubling issues it struggles with, feminist scholarship relies not only on its bourgeoning scholarship but on other important acquisitions. Despite the public skepticism about feminism, many of its central precepts are widely accepted; professors often face classes where the students bring some basic but often unacknowledged feminism to their studies. One of the strengths of feminist scholarship is that it ensures a population of women and men who know about sexism and who have learned about the history of struggles for women's equality and liberation. They are alert and ready to guard against attacks and backlashes. More importantly, many of them take feminist perspectives for granted and insist that other classes and the world engage seriously with feminism. Finally, by 2010, while it is still vulnerable, feminist scholarship is well-established globally. There were more than 900 women's/gender/feminist studies programs with websites worldwide and even more programs not yet on the web (Korenman 2010). In Canada, a group of high school girls initiated the Miss G Project, an organising effort to have women's studies recognized as a teachable subject in high school (see <http://www.themissgproject.org/>). Feminism's engagement with formal knowledge systems is powerful and sustained.

Conclusions: Why Feminism? Why Women's Studies?

The challenges posed by the vitriolic anti-feminist attacks that claim feminist scholarship is illegitimate because of its political aspects or discriminatory because it privileges women pose the questions: Why feminist scholarship? Why women's studies? And, in its more belligerent form, why not men's studies? From very different perspectives, some feminists and gender scholars pose similar questions in relation to the exclusions potentially implied by the focus on women: Why not gender or sexuality studies? How does the feminist focus on women relate to class, race, ethnicity, sexual orientation and sexuality and the various area studies that take up those concerns, such as Black, labour or social justice studies? What is the current justification for feminist studies? We think the answer to those questions is clear. The original problem, that feminist scholarship and women's studies were developed to confront, remains. Despite all the gains women have made, sexist discrimination remains, both in Canada and globally. Opposition to feminist knowledge, especially in the form of chilly indifference or the insidious insistence that because women now apparently have equality, special services for women can be cut, is still alive and well in universities, professional organizations and governments.

Women and the men who supported them fought for feminist scholarship so that women could do intellectual work and contribute to formal knowledge production as elite men had done for centuries. In Canada, that victory seems close. The struggle now is to make education available to all women and men, particularly in Aboriginal, rural, racialized and immigrant communities.[8] It is also to offer support and solidarity to those who still have to fight for women's access to education and for the possibilities of feminist scholarship around the world. But the struggle for greater economic, social and political power for women and for greater equality with men continues in Canada, as elsewhere. Despite the significant gains that have particularly benefited elite and professional white women, there are still significant inequalities (Statistics Canada 2010). Those inequalities are illustrated by a few examples.

In Canada, women still earn less than men and are more likely to be poor, especially if they have young children. Women on average earn 65 percent of what men earn; women working full time and full year earn 71 percent of what men working full time and full year earn (Statistics Canada 2010). Women have gained access to many occupations but are still excluded from the top paying and decision-making positions in most occupations. Only 6.9 percent of the most senior corporate offices are held by women (QMI Agency 2010) and only 16 women are CEOs of the top 500 corporations (Catalyst 2010). They also tend to be clustered in the lowest paying jobs in the clerical, sales and service sectors (Ferrao and Williams 2010). In the 2010 parliament, women held only 22.1 percent of seats in the House of

Commons, considerably less than the 30 percent minimum considered by the U.N. to be necessary to ensure a critical mass of women. Canada ranks forty-ninth internationally (with Mauritania), in the representation of women in the lower house of parliament. Visible minority women and Aboriginal women are even further underrepresented (Cool 2010).

Globally, the evidence is even more compelling. According to the United Nations report for 2010, *The World's Women,* women's access to education is still inadequate. One in four adults, or 876 million people in the world today are illiterate; that is, they cannot read or write. Two thirds of them are women, a proportion unchanged for more than two decades (United Nations 2010: 8). More than half of the 72 million children not in school are girls (United Nations 2010: 8) and women are less than 25 percent of all researchers world wide (United Nations 2010: 38). The long struggle for women's education continues.

In politics, there are about 192 recognized states; women are heads of state in only 11 of them. Globally, women are only 17 percent of elected MPs (United Nations 2010: 10). In some of the African states with new constitutions that take gender equality seriously, such as Rwanda, women make up 50 percent of all MPs. In the Nordic countries, which have explicit affirmative action policies, women hold 39 percent of elected MP positions. In the Americas, they hold 15 percent. In the Arabs states they hold 3.5 percent.

Economically, women make up 45 percent of the paid labour force around the world but their wages range from 20–50 percent less than men's. Fewer than 2 percent of top executive positions are held by women. Of the world's 500 largest corporations, only 13 have a woman CEO (United Nations 2010: 10). One billion people live in absolute poverty, which means they live on less than $1.00U.S. per day; 70 percent of them are women and girls. The U.N. estimates that, globally, between one third and one half of all women are abused.

The development of feminist scholarship and women's studies as an area of intellectual investigation, as a site of innovative, critical teaching and learning practices and as a legitimate academic and administrative unit in universities around the world, has been one moment in a long struggle for women's access to education in general, to universities in particular — an expression of the dream for women to become formal knowledge producers. That dream is central to the larger project of ensuring greater equality in all aspects of life for women compared to men and for all women and men.

Notes

1. "Formal knowledge systems" refers to the bodies of knowledge legitimated by the ruling powers, such as the intellectual, political and religious elites. In the Euro-North American tradition, since the thirteenth century, formal knowledge

production has been located mainly in universities (from which women were excluded until the late nineteenth century) and its history is one of contestation and struggle over what is recognized and accepted. Other forms of knowledge, articulated in popular culture, or in the ways of knowing of subordinated peoples, such as women, indigenous, colonized and working class people, are even more contested (Smith 1975, 1987; Hall 1981; Hill Collins 1990).

2.   For example, on December 3, 2010, the Executive Committee of the Canadian Sociological Association voted to merge the former Status of Women and Anti-Racism Sub-Committees into a new Equity Sub-Committee <http://www.csa-scs.ca/index.php?p=news>.

3.   Francine Decarriers maintains that French speaking feminists in Québec opted to work within existing disciplines to ensure that "le rapport des sexes" became central to each field (Robbins et al. 2008)

4.   Virginia Wolff [1929] (1984) said that what women need in order to write is a reliable income and "a room of one's own."

5.   Women's studies graduate students and faculty face similar difficulties when applying for research money from the Social Sciences and Humanities Research Council (SSHRC), the main source of funding for academic research. SSHRC refuses to recognize women's studies as a free-standing discipline, arguing that it is too small to warrant a committee of its own. Instead, they have combined women's studies with various other programs, at one point with nursing, currently with: communication, cultural studies and women's studies (committee 26) (SSHRC 2010). Women's studies scholars whose work doesn't readily fit with communication or cultural studies (studying legal practices, labour market trends or federal budgeting for example) face difficult choices about whether to apply to committee 26, or apply to disciplined-based committees, knowing many reviewers will know little about their field.

6.   As of December 2010, York University's Women's Studies program had fifty-two PhD graduates. UBC, Simon Fraser and the University of Ottawa had newer programs in which students are beginning to complete PhDs.

7.   For a critique of U.S. intellectuals from a right-wing perspective, see Sowell 2009.

8.   While the rates of participation in education for women and men are closer than ever, many woman and men still have limited or no access. In 2008, 84.2 percent of university teachers were white, 1 percent were Aboriginal, 1.6 percent Black (CAUT 2010: 20).

References

Adamson, Nancy, Linda Briskin, and Margaret McPhail. 1989. *Feminist Organizing for Change: The Contemporary Women's Movement in Canada.* Toronto: Oxford University Press.

Armstrong, Pat, and Roberta Hamilton. 1988. "Feminist Scholarship." *Canadian Review of Sociology and Anthropology* (25th Anniversary Issue) 25, 2 (May): 157–62.

Atlantis: A Women's Studies Journal. 1990. Special issue on women's studies professors. XVI, 1.

Bondy, Renee. 2010. "Women's Studies" *Herizons* Fall, 23 November <http://www.

herizons.ca/node/439>.

Boxer, Marilyn Jacoby. 1998. *When Women Ask the Questions: Creating Women's Studies in America*. Baltimore: Johns Hopkins University Press.

Briskin, Linda. 1990. *Feminist Pedagogy: Teaching and Learning Liberation*. Ottawa, ON: CRIAW/ICREF.

___. 2002. "Women's Organizing: A Gateway to a New Approach for Women's Studies." *Atlantis* 26, 2: 78–91.

Catalyst. 2010. "Women CEOs and Heads of the Financial Post 500." <www.catalyst. org/publication/322/women-ceos-of-the-fortune-1000>.

Clancy, James 2010. "NUPGE Condemns Tory Attack on Status of Women Canada." National Union of Public and General Employees, Ottawa <http://www.nupge. ca/news_2006/n24oc06b.htm>.

Cohen, Marjorie, and Ruth Roach Pierson (eds.). 1995. *Canadian Women's Issues, Vol. II, Bold Visions.* Halifax: Lorimer.

Cohen, Marjorie, Ruth Roach Pierson, Paula Bourne, and Philinda Masters (eds.). 1993. *Canadian Women's Issues, Vol. I, Strong Voices*. Halifax: Lorimer.

Cool, Julie. 2010. "Women in Parliament." Social Affairs Division, Parliamentary Information and Research Service, Library of Parliament, Publication No. 05-62E Revised 14 July. <http://www2.parl.gc.ca/content/lop/researchpublica-tions/prb0562-e.htm#a2>.

Dubinsky, Karen. 1985. *Lament for a Patriarchy Lost Anti-Feminism, Anti-Abortion and REAL Women in Canada*. Ottawa: Canadian Research Institute for the Advancement of Women.

Eichler, Margrit. 1981. "Power, Dependency, Love and the Sexual Division of Labour: A Critique of the Decision-Making Approach to Family Power and an Alternative Approach with an Appendix: On Washing My Dirty Linen in Public." *Women's Studies International Quarterly* 4, 2: 201–19

___. 1985. "And the Work Never Ends: Feminist Contributions." *Canadian Review of Sociology and Anthropology* 22.

Ferguson, Moira. 1985. *First Feminists: British Women Writers 158–1799* Bloomington: Indiana University Press.

Ferrao, Vincent, and Cara Williams. 2010. *Women in Canada: A Gender-Based Statistical Report*. 6th edition. Ottawa: Statistics Canada. Catelogue no. 89-503-XWE. <http://www.statcan.gc.ca/bsolc/olc-cel/olc-cel?catno=89-503-X&lang=eng>.

Franklin, Ursula, Michèle Jean, Syliva Van Kirk, Andrea Lebowitz, Meg Luxton, Susan Sherwin, and Dorothy Smith. 1984. *Knowledge Reconsidered: A Feminist Overview/Le Savoir en Question: Vue d'Ensemble Féministe*. Canadian Research Institute for the Advancement of Women, Ottawa.

Guettel, Charnie. 1974. *Marxism and Feminism*. Toronto: Canadian Women's Educational Press.

Hall, Stuart. 1981. "Notes on Deconstructing the Popular." In Raphael Samuel (ed.), *People's History and Socialist Theory*. London: Routledge Kegan Paul.

Hawkesworth, Mary. 2004. "The Semiotics of Premature Burial: Feminism in a Postfeminist Age." *Signs: Journal of Women in Culture and Society* 29, 4.

Hill Collins, Patricia. 1990. *Black Feminist Thought: Knowledge, Consciousness, and the Politics of Empowerment*. Boston: UnwinHyman.

Jacobson, Joyce. 2007. *The Economics of Gender* Malden, MA: Blackwell.

Jaggar, Alison, and Paula Rosenberg (eds.). 1993. *Feminist Frameworks: Alternative Theoretical Accounts of the Relations between Women and Men.* New York: McGraw-Hill.

Jean, Michele. 1984. "Creating and Communicating Knowledge from a Feminist Perspective: The Risks and Challenges for Women." In Ursula Franklin, Michele Jean, Sylvia Van Kirk, Andrea Lebowitz, Meg Luxton, Susan Sherwin, and Dorothy E. Smith, *Knowledge Reconsidered: A Feminist Overview/Le Savoir en Question: Vue d'Ensemble Féministe.* Ottawa: Canadian Research Institute for the Advancement of Women.

Korenman, Joan. 2010. "Women's Studies Programs, Departments, and Research Centres." <http://userpages.umbc.edu/~korenman/wmst/programs.html>.

Lerner, Gerda. 1997. *Why History Matters: Life and Thought.* Oxford University Press.

Lorde, Audre. 1984. *Sister Outsider: Essays and Speeches by Audre Lorde.* Trumansburg, NY: Crossing Press Feminist Series.

Loyd, Genevive. 1984. *The Man of Reason: "Male" and "Female" in Western Philosophy.* Minneapolis: MN University of Minnesota Press.

Luxton, Meg. 1984. "Conceptualizing 'Women' in Anthropology and Sociology." In Ursula Franklin, Michèle Jean, Sylvia Van Kirk, Andrea Lebowitz, Meg Luxton, Susan Sherwin, and Dorothy E. Smith, *Knowledge Reconsidered: A Feminist Overview/ Le Savoir en Question: Vue d'Ensemble Féministe* Ottawa: Canadian Research Institute for the Advancement of Women.

MacDonald, Eleanor. 1998. "Critical Identities: Rethinking Feminism through Transgender Politics." *Atlantis: A Women's Studies Journal* 23, 1 (Fall/Winter): 3–12.

Maroney, Heather Jon, and Meg Luxton. 1987. *Feminism and Political Economy: Women's Work, Women's Struggles.* Toronto: Methuen.

McDonald, Lynn (ed.). 1998. *Women Theorists on Society and Politic.s* Waterloo, ON: Wilfred Laurier University Press.

Messer-Davidow, Ellen. 2000. *Disciplining Feminism: From Social Activism to Academic Discourse.* Durham, NC: Duke University Press.

Mohanty, Chandra Talpade. 2003. *Feminism Without Borders: Decolonizing Theory, Practicing Solidarity.* Durham, NC: Duke University Press

National Post. 2010. "Women's Studies Is Still With Us." Editorial, 26 January: A12

O'Barr, Jean Fox. 1994. *Feminism in Action: Building Institutions and Community Through Women's Studies.* Chapel Hill, NC: University of North Carolina Press.

Paludi, Michele, and Gertrude Steuernagel. 1990. *Foundations for a Feminist Restructuring of the Academic Disciplines.* Binghamton, NY: Haworth Press.

Parry, S.C. 1996. "Feminist Pedagogy and Techniques for the Changing Classroom." *Women's Studies Quarterly* 24 (3 & 4): 45–54.

QMI Agency. 2010. "Fewer Women CEOs, but Blame the Recession: Report." <http://money.canoe.ca/money/business/canada/archives/2010/01/20100127-134920>.

Rowbotham, Sheila. 1972. *Women: Resistance and Revolution* London: Penguin.

___. 1973. *Women's Consciousness, Man's World.* London: Pelican Press.

___. 1992. *Women in Movement: Feminism and Social Action* London: Routledge.

Segal, Lynne. 1999. *Why Feminism? Gender, Psychology, Politics.* London: Polity.

Sherwin, Susan.1984. "From Feminism to a New Conception of Ethics." In Ursula Franklin, Michèle Jean, Sylvia Van Kirk, Andrea Lebowitz, Meg Luxton, Susan Sherwin, and Dorothy E. Smith, *Knowledge Reconsidered: A Feminist Overview/Le Savoir en Question: Vue d'Ensemble Féministe.* Ottawa: Ottawa: Canadian Research Institute for the Advancement of Women.

Smith, Dorothy. 1975. "An Analysis of Ideological Structures and How Women are Excluded." *The Canadian Review of Sociology and Anthropology* 12, 4 (pt. 1): 367.

___. 1984. "The Renaissance of Women Knowledge Reconsidered: A Feminist Overview." In Ursula Franklin, Michèle Jean, Sylvia Van Kirk, Andrea Lebowitz, Meg Luxton, Susan Sherwin, and Dorothy E. Smith, *Knowledge Reconsidered: A Feminist Overview/Le Savoir en Question: Vue d'Ensemble Féministe* Ottawa: Canadian Research Institute for the Advancement of Women.

___. 1987. *The Everyday World as Problematic: A Feminist Sociology.* Toronto: University of Toronto Press.

Sowell, Thomas. 2009. *Intellectuals and Society.* New York: Basic Books.

SSHRC. 2010. "SSHRC Research Standard Grants." <http://www.sshrc-crsh.gc.ca/funding-financement/peer_review-evaluation_pairs/selection_committees-comites_selection/standard_research-ordinaire_recherche-eng.aspx>.

Statistics Canada. 2010. "Women in Canada: Economic Well-Being." *The Daily.* 16 December. <http://www.statcan.gc.ca/daily-quotidien/101216/dq101216c-eng.htm>.

Thompson, William. [1828] 1983. *Appeal of One Half of the Human Race, Women, Against the Pretensions of the Other Half, Men, to Retain Them in Political and thence in Civil and Domestic Slavery.* London: Virago.

United Nations Secretariat, Department of Economic and Social Affairs. 2010. "The World's Women 2010 Trends and Statistics." NY 2010-11-22. <http://unstats.un.org/unsd/demographic/products/Worldswomen/WW_full%20 report_color.pdf>.

Van Kirk, Silvia. 1984. "What Has the Feminist Perspective Done for Canadian History?" In Ursula Franklin, Michèle Jean, Sylvia Van Kirk, Andrea Lebowitz, Meg Luxton, Susan Sherwin, and Dorothy E. Smith, *Knowledge Reconsidered: A Feminist Overview/Le Savoir en Question: Vue d'Ensemble Féministe.* Ottawa: Canadian Research Institute for the Advancement of Women.

Winkler, Barbara Scott, and Carolyn DiPalma (eds.). 1999. *Teaching Introduction to Women's Studies: Expectations and Strategies.* Westport, CY: Bergin and Garvey.

Wollstonecraft, Mary. [1792] 1967. *A Vindication of the Rights of Woman.* New York: Norton.

Woolf, Virginia [1929] 1994. *A Room of One's Own.* London, Flamingo.

___. 1939. *Three Guineas.* <http://www.feministezine.com/feminist/books/Virginia-Woolf-Three-Guineas.html>.

Yalnizyan, Armine. 2010. *The Rise of Canada's Richest 1%.* Ottawa: Canadian Centre for Policy Alternatives.

Chapter Two

CARTOGRAPHIES OF KNOWLEDGE AND POWER
Transnational Feminism as Radical Praxis

M. Jacqui Alexander and Chandra Talpade Mohanty

This chapter is one moment in the process of almost two decades of think-ing, struggling, writing and working together in friendship and solidarity as immigrant women of colour living in North America.[1] Each of us has been involved in collaborative work in and outside the academy in different racial, cultural and national sites — and we have worked together in scholarly, cur-ricular, institutional and organizing contexts. For us, this collaboration, over many years and in these many sites, has been marked by struggle, joy and the ongoing possibility of new understandings and illumination that only collective work makes possible.[2]

More than a decade ago, we embarked on a feminist collaborative project that resulted in the collection *Feminist Genealogies, Colonial Legacies, Democratic Futures* (Routledge 1997). Its main purpose was to take account of some of the most egregious effects of the political economic impact of globalization, what we called then capitalist recolonization — the racialized and gendered relations of rule of the state — both its neocolonial and ad-vanced capitalist incarnations, and to foreground a set of collective political practices that women in different parts of the world had undertaken as a way of understanding genealogies of feminist political struggles and orga-nizing. Our methodological task here was quite steep for the inheritance of the "international" within women's studies, particularly its U.S. variant, provided little analytic room to map the specific deployment of transnational that we intended *Feminist Genealogies* to encapsulate, especially since we saw that the term "international" had come to be collapsed into the cultures and values of capitalism and into notions of global sisterhood. How, then, could we conceptualize transnational to take globalization seriously while at the same time not succumb to the pitfalls of either free market capitalism or free market feminism?

Feminist Genealogies drew attention to three important elements in our definition of transnational: 1) a way of thinking about women in similar contexts across the world, in different geographical spaces, rather than as all women across the world; 2) an understanding of a set of unequal relationships among and between peoples, rather than as a set of traits embodied in all non-U.S. citizens (particularly because U.S. citizenship continues to be premised within a white, Eurocentric, masculinist, heterosexist regime); and 3) a consideration of the term "international" in relation to an analysis of economic, political and ideological processes that would therefore require taking critical antiracist, anticapitalist positions that would make feminist solidarity work possible (1997: xix).

In the decade since the publication of *Feminist Genealogies*, there has been a proliferation of discourses about transnational feminism, as well as the rise of transnational feminist networks.[3] Within the academy, particular imperatives like study abroad programs in different countries, the effects of Structural Adjustment Programs on public education globally, the (now lopsided) focus on area studies in geographical spaces seen as crucial to knowledge production post 9/11, and the rise of new disciplines like terrorism studies and security studies can all be read as responses to globalization that have concrete transnational contours. Transnational studies in the academy often dovetail with more radical impulses in social movements, and given the place of transnational feminist studies in the academy at this moment, we have embarked on another large collaborative project, this time seeking to map a genealogy or archeology of the transnational in feminist and LGBTT/queer studies in the United States and Canada.

To this end we pose a set of questions that can probe the definitions of transnational feminism in relation to globalization (local/global/regional) and the operation of the categories of gender, race, nation, sexuality and capitalism. We want to explore what the category of the transnational il- luminates — the work it does in particular feminist contexts — the relation of the transnational to colonial, neocolonial and imperial histories and practices on different geographical scales, and finally we want to analyze the specific material and ideological practices that constitute the transnational at this historical juncture and in the U.S. and Canadian sites we ourselves occupy. When is the transnational a normativizing gesture — and when does it perform a radical, decolonizing function? Are cultural relativist claims smuggled into the transnational in ways that reinforce binary notions of tradition and modernity?

A number of feminist scholars have distinguished between the categories of global, international and transnational. Suzanne Bergeron (2001), for instance, argues that globalization is the condition under which transna- tional analysis is made possible. The transnational is connected to neoliberal economics and theories of globalization — it is used to distinguish between the global as a universal system, and the cross-national, as a way to engage the interconnections between particular nations. Feminist scholars have also defined the transnational in relation to women's cross-border organizing (Mindry 2001) and as a spatialized analytic frame that can account for varying scales of representation, ideology, economics and politics, while maintaining a commitment to difference and asymmetrical power. Radcliffe et al. (2003), for instance, connect the transnational to the neoliberal through exchanges of power that impact indigenous communities across the globe. Felicity Schaeffer-Gabriel (2006) defines the current form of economics in relation to ideologies of masculinity, examining what she refers to as the "transnational routes of U.S. masculinity."

Our own definitions of transnational feminist praxis are anchored in very particular intellectual and political genealogies — in studies of race, colonialism and empire in the global North, in the critiques of feminists of colour in the U.S., and in studies of decolonization, anticapitalist critique and LGBTT/queer studies in the North and the South. Our use of this category is thus anchored in our own locations in the global North, and in the commitment to work systematically and overtly against racialized, heterosexist, imperial, corporatist projects that characterize North American global adventures. We are aware that this particular genealogy of the transnational is specific to our locations and the materiality of our everyday lives in North America. Here our interest lies in the connections between the politics of knowledge, and the spaces, places and locations that we occupy. Our larger project, then, is an attempt to think through the political and epistemological struggles that are embedded in radical transnational feminist praxis at this time.

For this chapter, however, we focus on a particular part of this larger project. Drawing on an analysis of the contemporary U.S. academy and on core women's and gender studies and LGBTT/queer studies syllabi, we attempt a preliminary map of the institutional struggles over transnational feminist praxis, specifically, the politics of knowledge construction in women's studies and LGBTT/queer studies in the U.S. academy. Given the privatization and restructuring of the U.S. academy, the hegemony of neoliberalism and corporate/capitalist values and free market ideologies, the increasingly close alignment of the academy with the "war on terror" and the U.S. imperial project, we ask questions about the objects of knowledge involved in women's and gender studies and LGBTT/queer studies. Beginning with a broad mapping of the U.S. academy as a major site in the production of knowledge about globalization and the transnational, we move on to an analysis of the ethics and politics of knowledge in the teaching of transnational feminism. The two fundamental questions that preoccupy us are: What are the specific challenges for collaborative transnational feminist praxis given the material and ideological sites that many of us occupy? And, what forms of struggle engender cultures of dissent and decolonized knowledge practices in the context of radical transnational feminist projects? We believe that at this historical moment it is necessary to move away from the academic/activist divides that are central to much work on globalization, to think specifically about destabilizing such binaries through formulations of the spatialization of power and to recall the genealogy of public intellectuals, radical political education movements and public scholarship that is anchored in cultures of dissent. Such work also requires acute ethical attentiveness. In addressing herself to the African Studies Association in 2006, Amina Mama (2007: 3) speaks of the need for developing scholarship as a "critical tradition premised on an ethic of freedom." She goes on to define this:

> Such scholarship regards itself as integral to the struggle for freedom and holds itself accountable, not to a particular institution, regime, class or gender, but to the imagination, aspirations and interests of ordinary people. It is a tradition some would call radical, as it seeks to be socially and politically responsible in more than a neutral or liberal sense.

Thus, one of the major points of our analysis is to understand the relationship between a politics of location and accountability, and the politics of knowledge production by examining the academy as one site in which transnational feminist knowledge is produced, while examining those knowledges that derive from political mobilizations that push up, in and against the academy ultimately foregrounding the existence of multiple genealogies of radical transnational feminist practice.

The U.S. Academy: Mapping Location and Power

The U.S. academy is a very particular location for the production of knowledge. Within a hegemonic culture of conformity and surveillance, many of us experience the perils of being in the U.S. academy. At a time when women's and gender studies, race and ethnic studies, queer studies and critical area studies run the risk of co-optation within the neoliberal, multiculturalist, corporatist frame of the academy, we bear a deep responsibility to think carefully and ethically about our place in this academy where we are paid to produce knowledge, and where we have come to know that the spatiality of power needs to be made visible and to be challenged. One of the questions we want to raise, then, is whether it is possible to undo the convergence between location and knowledge production. Put differently, can transnational feminist lenses push us to ask questions that are location specific but not necessarily location bound? If we take seriously the mandate to do collaborative work in and outside the academy, the kind of work that would demystify the borders between inside and outside and thereby render them porous rather than mythically fixed, it is imperative that the academy not be the only location that determines our research and pedagogical work;

that we recognize those hierarchies of place within the multiple sites and locations in which knowledge is produced, and we maintain clarity about the origin of the production of knowledge and the spaces where this knowledge travels. And this mandate in turn requires the recognition that knowledge is produced by activist and community-based political work — that some knowledges can only emerge within these contexts and locations. Thus, in not understanding the intricate and complex links between the politics of location, the geographies and spatialities of power and the politics of knowledge production, we risk masking the limits of the work we do within the academy and more specifically their effects on the kinds of pedagogic projects we are able to undertake in the classroom. We attempt to clarify and address some of these links in the second half of this essay. Our intention here is not to reinforce or solidify an academic/activist divide, although we are well aware that these divides exist. It is rather to draw attention to different academic and activist sites as differentiated geographies of knowledge production. Thus, we want to be attentive to the spatialities of power and the ways in which they operate in and though the academy, as well as within political movements whose identities are not constituted within it.

In North America, the binary that distinguishes the "academy" from the "community" or the academic from the activist, that has also made it necessary to pen the qualification "activist scholar," has assisted in the creation of apparently distinct spaces where the former is privileged over the latter. This process or binary/boundary making is also a fundamental way to (re)configure space and to mask the power relations that constitute that reconfiguration. We can think of this binary as spatial in that it has its own cartographic rules, which, according to Katherine McKittrick, "unjustly organize human hierarchies *in place* and reify uneven geographies in familiar, seemingly natural ways" (McKittrick 2006: xiv, emphasis in original). Given over two decades of neoliberalism, privatization and the accompanying commodification of knowledge that marks academies across the globe, the cartographic rules of the academy necessarily produce insiders and outsiders in the geographies of knowledge production. On the one hand, such cartographic rules draw somewhat rigid boundaries around neoliberal academies (the academy/community divide), and on the other they normalize the spatial location of the academy as the epitome of knowledge production. So what are these cartographic rules that normalize the position of the academy at the pinnacle of this knowledge-making hierarchy? Among them are the making of white heterosexual masculinity consonant with the identity of the institution against which racialized and sexed others are made, imagined and positioned as well as the diffusion of ways of knowing that are informed by the fictions of European Enlightenment rationality, which heighten political contestation from those knowledges that are made to bear an oppositional genealogy and are rendered marginal once they travel inside the academy. These rules are reinforced through an ideological apparatus that creates the academy/community divide in the first place and that is itself an element in the deployment of power while attempting to conceal that power through other border patrol strategies such as: academic-community partnerships and the creation of various offices of community relations; and devising strategies of governance that delimit the kind of scholar and the kind of scholarship deserving legitimation, which are at odds with the very community with which it has established relations.[4] These cartographic rules are crucial since they create a hierarchy of place and permit the binary to operate as a verb, demarcating the spurious divide between academy and community while at the same time masking the creation of the divide. We say spurious here not because the creation of boundaries does not have serious effects in creating insiders and outsiders along lines similar to those created by the state, for instance, but because the practices of power within the academy bear close resemblance to the practices of power deployed by its allies such as the state and global capital that participate both materially and ideologically in its day-to-day operation. Ultimately these rules promote a spatial segregation that constructs the "community" as a hyper-racialized homogeneous space; and it is usually not just any community but one that has been subject to forced dispossession. This community may or may not be the same as grassroots mobilizations that derive from many sources. To make visible, then, these racialized geographies of dispossession with their own imperatives that do not rely on the academy for self-definition even as the academy summons them, and reifies them in that summoning, in the service of the formation of its own identity is a crucial strategy. This gesture assists us in demystifying the cartographic rules, fragmenting the hierarchy of place that would make them an undifferentiated mass in relation to the academy and thus in identifying the operation of the very idea of the spatialization of power that points to the social formation of multiple uneven spaces, which individually and together make up the power/knowledge matrix. Who resides in which spaces? Who belongs and who are rendered outsiders? Who is constituted as the knowledgeable and the unknowledgeable? Which knowledges and ways of knowing are legitimized and which are discounted? Settling these questions stands at the core in making hierarchies of place.

This power/knowledge matrix that creates insiders and outsiders, those who know and those who cannot know, has of course been challenged in multiple spaces by edu-activists. Two examples of political movements that challenge the cartographic rules consolidated by neoliberal, privatized academies include the Committee on Academic Freedom in Africa (CAFA) and the Italian Network for Self-Education founded in 2005. CAFA, founded in 1991, mobilized North American students and teachers in support of African edu-activists fighting against World Bank-initiated Structural Adjustment Programs (SAPs) aimed at dismantling autonomous African university systems. Arguing that these SAP initiatives were part of a larger attack on African workers, and that they functioned as recolonization projects, CAFA drew attention to the inexorable dismantling of African higher education resulting in the shift of knowledge production elsewhere from international NGOs training technocrats under the "African Capacity Building" initiative to U.S. international and study abroad programs. Similarly, the Italian Network for Self-Education was formed in 2005 as a result of a mass mobilization of over 150,000 people in response to the restructuring of academic labour by the Italian parliament. Challenging the spatialization of knowledge and expertise within disciplines, faculties and the logic of neoliberal university systems, the network claims to traverse the division between teaching and research, education and metropolitan production and theory and praxis. The self-education movement deconstructs traditional modes of knowledge production and research, unsettling the taken-for-granted cartographic binary of the university/metropole, potentially serving as a device for social transformation.[5] Thus, the spatialities of power that anoint the academy as the pinnacle of knowledge are demystified and profoundly challenged by CAFA and the Network for Self-Education.

For our purposes, however, and in order to wrestle with the gendered, racialized and sexualized spatialization of power, we would have to come to terms with what McKittrick (2006) calls its material physicality, which, in the context of this chapter, pertains to our own formulations of the objects of transnational feminist analysis and the potential cartographic rules of syllabi, the spaces where colonialism and race dovetail with the practices of empire, where the academy consorts with state and corporatist projects and where oppositional practices take hold in ways that bend those cartographic rules or make them situationally irrelevant to the practices or hegemonic power. Those physical spaces include: the detention centre; the army, the navy and other institutions of the military-industrial complex; the institutions of state; the corporation, the factory, the export processing zones, the warehouse for secondhand clothing, the home, the brothel; the capsized boat, makeshift homes, the desert; the neighborhood, the street, NGOs, cross-border networks; the university, the boardroom, the classroom.[6] The question we want to ask then is, under what conditions, and for what purpose do particular spaces become dominant in the construction of the transnational?

Almost two decades ago, Jonathan Feldman, Noam Chomsky and others analyzed the role of the academy in what was then referred to as the military-industrial complex (Feldman 1989). In 2008, the academy continues to figure prominently in the consolidation of Empire, the corporatization of knowledge and the operation of the national security state. Most visibly, it aids in the surveillance and policing functions of the state via the *USA Patriot Act* of 2001, which calls for international students, scholars and their dependents on F and J visas to be registered on SEVIS, a web-based data collection and monitoring system created to link the academy to the Department of Homeland Security, consulates and embassies abroad, ports of entry into the United States and other state agencies. The intimate connections between scientific knowledge, corporate power and profit have now been examined by many scholars.[7] And the earlier discussion of CAFA and the Network for Self-Education points to radical educational movements that challenge the corporatization of the academy and its varied geographies of power in different national spaces.

The social organization of knowledge in the academy, its structures of inquiry and discipline-based pedagogies are inevitably connected to larger state and national projects. And this is nowhere more palpable as in the mobilization of various disciplines, beyond area studies, to assist the state in the consolidation of empire.[8] They engender their own complicities as well as practices of dissent. Just as privatized academies engender capitalist, market-based citizenship, they also encode stories of the U.S. nation — a presumably "democratic" nation that is simultaneously involved in the project of empire building. One important aspect of a radical transnational feminist project then involves looking at the way curricula and pedagogies mark and become sites for the mobilization of knowledge about the transnational. In what follows we examine syllabi in women's and gender studies (WGS), and in LGBTT/queer studies, in an attempt to understand the deployment of the transnational. Given our focus on the spatialization of power, we look especially at how those WGS and LGBTT/queer studies syllabi that deploy the transnational organize a set of cartographic rules that define how knowledge production operates in the academy. We look at syllabi in terms of the racial and gendered spatialization of power. This suggests questions like what kinds of hierarchies of place and space get set up; how power gets configured and reiterated; where do teachers locate feminism and queer sexuality in relation to these larger processes of colonialism and imperialism; the organization and presence of the academy and grassroots activism, political mobilizations, and so forth. Put differently, in what ways do syallbi bend or reinforce normative cartographic rules?

The Politics of Feminist Knowledge: Curricular Maps and Stories

The ethics and politics of crossing cultural, geographical and conceptual borders in feminist and LGBTT/queer pedagogies in the context of the transnational is a crucial element in analyzing the interface of the politics of knowledge and location in the academy. How we teach transnational feminism in women's studies is crucial in analyzing the struggles over knowledge and power both within the U.S. academy and outside its fictive borders. The way we construct curricula and the pedagogies we use to put such curricula in to practice tell a story — or tell many stories of gendered, racial and sexual bodies in work and home spaces, prisons and armed forces, boardrooms and NGOs, local and transnational organizations and so on. We suggest that these "stories" are also anchored in cartographic rules that encapsulate differentiated and hierarchical spatialities, thus foregrounding the links between sites, location and the production of knowledge about the transnational. "Stories" are simultaneously "maps" in that they mobilize both histories and geographies of power. Thus, just as we suggested there are cartographic rules that normalize the position of the academy in the knowledge hierarchy earlier, we now explore whether similar rules are encoded and normalized in the curriculum, specifically in the syllabi we analyze.

We analyze thirteen core syllabi from WGS and LGBTT/queer studies curricula at a variety of colleges and universities in the United States in terms of these stories and maps. The sample syllabi we chose were from large state universities; private, elite universities; small liberal arts colleges; and smaller state schools.[9] Each of the syllabi gesture toward transnational feminist praxis in some form or another, and most seem to anchor the core curriculum in women's and gender and LGBTT/queer studies. We suggest that an examination of the core curriculum can help us understand the politics of knowledge and the spatialities of power in the cross-cultural construction of feminist and LGBTT/queer studies in the U.S. academy, and to ask questions about the academy as a site for such knowledge production. This analysis allows us to see what it is students are being asked to know within these disciplines at this historical moment and what knowledge is being generated within introductory and upper-level classrooms — those spaces where explicitly oppositional knowledges are being produced. It also allows us to make preliminary connections between the politics of location, differentiated spatializations and the production of knowledge.

Some of the larger analytic questions we might then ask include: How precisely is the transnational deployed in the core curriculum in relationship to racial and colonial histories and geographies, and to the relationship of the local and global? What happens with the transnational when it encounters women of colour, for instance, or queer communities of colour? What productive tensions and contradictions are visible when the transnational emerges? What cartographic rules pertaining to the transnational can be made visible in this analysis of syllabi? In what ways are curricular stories also curricular maps? And finally, are there convergences and/or divergences in the ways that these transnational maps intersect with the spatialization of power in the academy as a whole?

Specifically, we analyzed six syllabi designated as core introductory courses and seven upper-level courses in the interdisciplinary fields of WGS and LGBTT/queer studies. Examples of these include Introduction to Women's and Gender Studies, Introduction to LGBTT/Queer Studies and Introduction to Feminist Studies. We were interested in understanding what categories (for example, gender, race, nation and sexuality) animate the transnational, the work it is being called upon to do in the curriculum, the particular histories and spatialities (colonial, neocolonial, imperial) it mobilizes and the practices that are seen to constitute transnational feminism.

While our selection of these syllabi was intentional, purposive one might say, in that our explicit focus was the transnational, we should also note that there were many upper-level seminars devoted to an exploration of "urgent contemporary issues" of gender or of sexuality in which there was a curious elision of the transnational within the United States, pushing it to operate only elsewhere, outside of the geopolitical borders of the U.S. nation-state.[10] This paradoxical duality of marked absence on the one hand and of hyper-presence on the other might leave no way for students to negotiate the circuits of travel between the local and the global, or to intuit the precise ways in which the local is constituted through the global. Still, we have to leave open the possibility that such linkages are indeed made. We might, for instance, talk about this particular curricular strategy as the cartographic rule of the transnational as always "elsewhere." This "elsewhere" rule thus suggests a separation of the spaces of the local/national and the transnational.

Overall, the interweaving of the categories of racialized gender and sexuality as well as the attention to non-U.S. feminist geographies was impressive. In many of these courses, there was a marked shift from the ways in which racialized and cross-cultural knowledges were being produced in WGS courses in the 1970s and 1980s. Unlike in most WGS curricula from the 1970s and 1980s, women of colour texts, queer texts by men and women of colour from different parts of the world, and texts by "Third World" women are central in the syllabi we analyzed. Yet there were many paradoxes. In the case of LGBTT/queer studies, one of the most complex of the introductory syllabi exposed students to the lives and experiences of U.S. queer communities of colour, linking these with racialized colonial histories of immigrant and native communities and the contemporary effects of globalization. The central actors in this narrative were thus queers of colour and the conceptual movement of the course mapped sexuality studies in relation to colonialism, racial formation, nation-states and finally to globalization. Paradoxically, however, the central "stories" remained U.S.-centric with the U.S. being defined as a multicultural, multiracial nation in the most interesting of these syllabi. Here is yet another cartographic rule then, one that constructs a hierarchy of place within the transnational: the U.S.- or Eurocentric organization of the syllabus. However, this is very different from the "elsewhere" rule in that it suggests a connectivity of the spaces of the local/national, and the trans-national, but always in terms of a hierarchy of place wherein Euro-America constitutes the norm.

Genealogies of sexuality studies remain largely U.S.-centred in otherwise multiple-layered courses. Thus, while racial and colonial histories were often threaded through the courses, these histories remained focused on the U.S. or Europe. In one Introduction to LGBTT/Queer Studies course, designed as an introduction to the academic interdisciplinary field itself, the syllabus drew on the now familiar canon of theorists of sexuality (Foucault, Sedgwick, Butler), yet again mobilizing Euro-American histories of sexuality while referring to the lives and experiences of queer communities of colour.

This paradox of foregrounding subjects of colour as agents while repro-ducing a white Eurocentric centre has another effect in that the transnational can be deployed in normative rather than critical terms. In one upper-level seminar, the story of the syllabus was to map the impact of globalization on different women in different parts of the world.[11] Marking this difference is clearly important since it moves us away from thinking of globalization as a homogenous or homogenizing project. Yet the emphasis on democratization and equality as a way to understand feminist mobilizations among Islamic, Latin American or African feminists seemed to perform an odd theoretical move that wished to export democracy and equality from the U.S. to these different parts of the world. Ironically, the syllabus carried a great deal of resonance with earlier formulations of a global sisterhood, though it did so in terms that were ostensibly different: the terms of "multiple feminisms." Indeed residing underneath these multiple feminisms was cultural relativism that housed two interrelated elements. One was the creation of a geographic distance through which an absolute alterity was constructed. It was only through greater proximity to the United States and the inherited categories of the West that women's experiences were most intelligible. The other, implied in the first, was the spatial creation of an *us* and *them* so that Islamic, Latin American or African feminism could neither be understood relationally nor could they be positioned to interrogate the kinds of feminist mobilizations deployed in the West.[12] The place of Western knowledge was reconsolidated all over again. Here, too, while spatial connectivities are mobilized, there is a clear hierarchy in place.

Our analysis suggests several important trends. First, in spite of its link to racial and colonial histories, the transnational is made to inhabit very dif-ferent meanings and emerges at different junctures and in different spaces in the overall story of the syllabi we examined. Second, in the introductory courses to gender and sexuality where the writings and theorizations of U.S. women of colour and non-Western women's movements were central, the stories these syllabi dealt with were of complex feminisms anchored in different racial communities of women and queers. However, not only were U.S. and Eurocentric histories mobilized, for instance, the linear periodization of first-, second- and third-wave feminisms, but also very visible were the genealogies of feminist thought that once again foregrounded narratives of European liberal, socialist and postmodern theory. Cartographically, then, the transnational was either placed elsewhere or positioned Eurocentrically or within the United States as theoretically normative.

Transnational feminism also emerged in all of these courses in relation to singular and often isolated categories and contexts. Thus, for instance, it was made visible only in relation to discussions of work and globalization, or human rights, or gay diasporas, or cross-border mobilizations. The majority of the readings and topics of the syllabi remained U.S.-centric. Thus, transnationalism might emerge, for instance, only in relation to queer diasporas and the effects of globalization, with only two out of fourteen weeks devoted to "gay diasporas and queer transnationalism," rendering it an exceptional or theoretical option. In other words, the local remained intact, and somewhat disconnected from cross-border experiences. Transnationalism was then anchored only outside the borders of the nation (the "elsewhere" rule). Thus, it seems that the transnational has now come to occupy the place that race and women of colour held in women's studies syllabi in the 1990s and earlier. We have now moved from white women's studies to multiracial women's studies (in the best instances), but the methodology for understanding the transnational remains an "add and stir" method, and the maps that are drawn construct the transnational as spatializing power either "elsewhere" or as within the United States and/or Europe.

Thus, a focus on diaspora, globalization and colonial discourse as well as on feminist and LGBTT/queer communities in different national contexts often seems to stand in for what the courses describe as a "transnational perspective." Transnationalism, if identified at all, is understood only in the context of contemporary globalization or, in some rare cases, with nationalisms and religious fundamentalisms that fuel cross-border masculinist and heterosexist state practices. Given our interest in the politics of knowledge and the place of transnational feminisms in the academy, we were especially intrigued by the fact that none of these introductory courses raised questions about the ethics of cross-cultural knowledge production, or about the academy at all. This curious absence of the academy as the space many of us occupy every day, given the larger political battles that often shape our curricula and pedagogy seems all the more problematic from the point of view of understanding the spatiality of power in terms of the academy and its relationship to other institutions of rule like the state and corporate interests. After all, being attentive to the ethics of knowledge production requires bringing questions of identity, epistemology and method to the forefront of our scholarship and teaching. If the academy as a political space is absent from our syllabi, even as experience remains central to feminist thinking, surely there is a major contradiction here. We may be erasing our own experiences (and the profoundly material effects of our locations) at our own peril. For instance, as Amina Mama (2007: 6) argues, "our intellectual identities — and the ethics that we adopt to guide our scholarly practices — are informed by our identifications with particular communities and the values they uphold." Thus, if we take the connections between the politics of knowledge and the politics of location (identity) and of space seriously, we may need to take on broad institutional ethnography projects that allow a materialist understanding of academic spaces as mobilizing and reproducing hegemonic power. While some courses touched on urgent transnational issues like HIV/AIDS and war and militarism, there was no mention of the U.S. imperial project or, say, the prison industrial complex as a site of analysis or feminist debate, thus begging the question of what particular (transnational) issues women's and gender studies and LGBTT/queer studies curricula speak to in the world we now occupy. Interestingly then, syllabi may serve unwittingly to reinforce and even naturalize the university/community divide in terms of hierarchies of location, identity and sites of knowledge.

One upper-level seminar, however, was notable in terms of its explicit engagement with some of the ethical conundrums associated with cross-cultural comparison, which seemed crucial in light of its attention to the methodological politics of doing cross-cultural work. The story of this syllabus was a complex one, attempting to map the ways in which sex, sexuality and gender operated within local and global processes that are at once transnational since the rapid dispersal of peoples and reading and interpretive practices operated everywhere. Within the construction of "queer diaspora" and the making of queer historiography, the social actors were specific communities that included cultures of two-spirit, cross-dressing women in U.S. Civil War; the *fa'afafine* of Samoa; and gay, lesbian and transgender communities in different geographies, thus resisting the impulse to create a queer universal subject, and engendering a map that was attentive to different spatializations in the construction of sexualities. The syllabus asked explicit questions about when comparisons were useful or when they participated in reproducing the kind of discursive violence that comes with imposing U.S. social categories on cultural configurations that were not U.S.-based. It was also interested in having students see themselves as intellectuals with ethical responsibilities: "What is our responsibility," it asked, "as students of gender and sexuality studies to be aware of the politics of making 'queer' travel?" Thus, this particular syllabus also engaged partially with the U.S. academy as a contested site in the production of knowledge.

Finally, all of the upper-level seminars we examined signaled the transnational through some political economic pressures of globalization, diaspora and migration. Importantly, racial and colonial histories marked the transnational in all instances. For example, in one course the story of transnational feminism was one in which the politics of women of colour in the United States was linked to feminist movements among "Third World" women, attempting to map genealogies of feminism by asking how these feminisms had reshaped mainstream U.S. feminist praxis. While racialization functioned primarily in relationship to women of colour, transnational feminist theory seemed hesitant, however, to engage women of colour or "Third World Women" as sexual subjects or interpolated within sexualized projects pertaining to the state and/or global capital. Most often gender and sexuality were positioned either as theoretical strangers or distant cousins, once again reinforcing a separation of constructs of race and sexuality in the organization of knowledge about transnational feminisms.

This distancing of sexuality from questions of transnational feminism or rather the practice of deploying an uninterrogated heterosexuality within transnational feminist analyses both cedes the domain of sexuality to LGBTT/ queer studies and renders an incomplete story of the ways in which the racialized, gendered practices of neoimperial modernity are simultaneously sexualized. Some of the methodological cues for probing these links have been laid out by Jacqui in earlier work, where she stages a political conversation between transnational feminism and sexuality studies by examining the complicity of state and corporate practices in the manufacture of heterosexual citizenship and nation-building structures practices as seemingly disparate as welfare, structural adjustment and discursive legal practices such as Domestic Violence in the Caribbean, the *Defense of Marriage Act* and the Don't Ask Don't Tell policy of the U.S. military.[13] She suggests one possible analytic strategy by bringing these practices into ideological and geographical proximity to one another and by foregrounding heterosexual regulatory practices as those of violence. Thus, she is able to bring sexuality within the racialized, gendered practices of the state and capital both within and across formations that have been separately designated as colonial, neocolonial and neoimperial and conceive of the transnational across a wide range of ideological, political, economic and discursive practices straddling multiple temporalities and multiple interests. This question about the connectivity of multiple through unequally organized geographies, temporalities and interests bears on the question that is at the heart of our consideration, that is the relationship between the politics of location and the politics of knowledge production and who is able, that is, legitimized, to make sustainable claims about these links. And it raises additional questions about the analytic and political consequences of deploying an either/or framing: either connectivity or separation. Hierarchies of space and place mark what we have called the cartographic rules of the transnational in the syllabi we examined. Thus, while the transnational as elsewhere signals the spatial separation of sites of knowledge, the transnational as U.S.- or Eurocentric signals connectivity, but on the basis of a hierarchical spatialization of power.

Multiplying Radical Sites of Knowledge

Let's now consider the antiviolence and political mobilizations to abolish prisons that dovetail with antiglobalization and antimilitarization campaigns. Activists in these global networks have examined how punishment regimes, including the prison, are intimately linked to global capitalism, neoliberal politics and U.S. economic and military dominance (Sudbury 2005). More specifically, however, it is the incarceration of increasing numbers of impoverished women of colour that enables us to track the links between neoliberal privatization, the U.S. export of prison technologies, organized militarization, dominant and subordinate patriarchies and neocolonial ideologies. As Sudbury argues, "Women's testimonies of survival under neoliberal cutbacks, border crossing, exploitation in the sex and drug industries, and life under occupation and colonial regimes provide a map of the local and global factors that generate prison as a solution to the conflicts and social problems generated by the new world order" (xiii). One of those social problems is the massive migration of impoverished women and men from the global South instigated by neoliberal globalization, who are now disproportionately criminalized together with Indigenous and Aboriginal women from Canada and the United States to Australia.

Sudbury's collection, *Global Lockdown*, is significant for thinking through these relationships refracted through the transnational spatialization of power for several reasons. First, it is located within critical antiprison and antiviolence projects such as Critical Resistance, the Prison Activist Resource Centre, the Arizona Prison Moratorium Coalition and Social Justice. Second, the contributors to the collection, in Sudbury's words, are "intellectuals both organic and intellectual, former prisoners, political prisoners, activists, women in recovery, former sex workers, immigrants and indigenous women" (xi), who by virtue of their differentiated locations point to the gaps that ensue when political struggle is not attentive to connectivity. Third, to take seriously the insights of differently positioned intellectuals is not to argue that prison intellectuals or sex workers have knowledge too; rather it is to say that their location engenders an epistemic advantage that researchers not similarly positioned have been unable to mobilize. It helps us to explain why scholars "have yet to locate race, citizenship and national status at the centre of the prison boom" (xviii). And fourth, it enacts different border crossings of geography and the nation-state; of time and the continued, albeit discontinuous, traffic between the colonial, the neocolonial and the imperial; among and between different colonized spaces; of different yet related political mobilizations at the centre of whose praxis is the labour of building connectivity not only to upset the cartographic rules that would position the prison and the brothel as separate and unrelated spaces and the women within them only as "objects of scholarly study and state rehabilitation" (xxiv) but to redraw and therefore reiterate through practice the connectivity of those spaces and ultimately of the political struggles that make connectivity possible. What then is the ethical responsibility of the teacher in the university classroom who wishes to teach about globalization and privatization, militarization and the racialized gendered global lockdown?

If to talk about space is to talk also about geography, then to talk about geography is to talk also about land and the fierce contestations over land that are at the centre of both neoimperial and colonial land appropriation. And if we think the ways in which the colonial traffics in the neoimperial, then it becomes possible to delineate the many ways in which white settler colonization continues to be an important dimension of the spatialization of power at this very moment in history. It also explains why struggles for sovereignty and the retrieval of stolen lands figure so centrally in Aboriginal, First Nations and Indigenous politics.

Aboriginal, First Nations and Indigenous activists and scholars together have written and organized at the fragile border between the master histories of legislated inclusion and the always disappeared, the twin ideological companions of the material practices of genocide. Locating this matrix within the context of white supremacy, Andrea Smith (2006: 68, emphasis in original) has argued that "[the logic of genocide] holds that indigenous peoples must disappear. In fact they must *always* be disappearing in order to allow non-indigenous peoples' rightful claim over this land." In *Conquest*, Smith pulls from the lived experiences of Native Women to draw links between this disappearance and the organization of a colonial patriarchy that deployed sexual violence against Native women — and other women of colour — who were and continue to be positioned as "rapeable," and "violable," in much the same way in which land is appropriated, raped and violated. In this formulation, it is not so much elsewhere cartographic rule that is at work — elsewhere as in outside the boundaries of modernity — but rather absence, that "present absence," as Kate Shanley (cited in Smith 2006) calls it, which in this ideological script has presumably no knowledge to possess. Thus, fashioning political struggles in ways that refuse these contradictory divides provides insight into how and why struggles for sovereignty and for land are simultaneously political, physical and spatial, metaphysical and spiritual (LaDuke 2005; Pinto 2003). Of course one central question that emerges here has to do with the ways in which that disappearance in the colonial and imperial geography travels within the academy and manifests as negligible numbers of Native students, teachers and administrators and, as significantly, their disappearance in curricular and other pedagogical projects in the classroom.[14]

We noted earlier that the hierarchies of place position a community that is racially homogeneous and otherwise undifferentiated. But mapping community from an understanding of the differentiated and heterogeneous colonial spaces of "containment, internment and exile" (Burman 2007: 177) creates the possibility of a deeper and more nuanced understanding of the subjects who are positioned to stand outside of modernity, presumably outside of citizenship, displaced from land in the same way that, for instance, the "deportable subject," the "admissible subject," "the present absent subject," the suspect subject are positioned by the state against the exalted national subject (the term is Thobani's) within the segregated landscape of transnational modernity. It is the combined work of activists and scholars that has brought these meanings to our understanding of occupied territory within white settler states.

Thinking through the outlines of a radical feminist project at a time when U.S. imperialism, genocide, incarceration, militarization and empire building have significantly deepened is both tough and unnecessary.[15] While a "multiple feminisms" pedagogical strategy may be more analytically viable than the "Euro-American feminism as the normative subject" of feminist and LGBTT/queer studies curricula, the specter of cultural relativism remains intact. Transnational feminist solidarities and ethical cross-cultural comparisons attentive to the histories and hierarchies of power and agency cannot be premised on an "us and them" foundation. Our conceptual foci would need to shift and that might be possible when different cross-border practices, spaces and temporalities are brought into ideological and geographic proximity with one another in ways that produce connectivity and inter-subjectivity (albeit a tense or uneven one) rather than an absolute alterity. We would need to be attentive to how we think the object of our research, for what the antiprison/antiglobalization mobilizations suggest is that solidarity work provokes us to pay close attention to the spaces of confinement that warehouse those who are surplus or resistant to the new world order (Sudbury 2005: xii). "Multiple feminisms" would need to be anchored in ways of reading that foreground the ethics of knowledge production and political practices across multiple borders — both those that are hypervisible and those that are somewhat invisible — within hierarchies of domination and resistance. And questions of responsibility and accountability need to be central to this pedagogy, as do ethnographies of the academy as sites of struggle and contested spaces of knowledge.

What might a map of a radical, non-normative transnational feminist solidarity pedagogy that is attentive to the genealogies and spatializations of power across multiple borders look like? Clearly syllabi are crucial spaces for thinking the reconfiguring of knowledge, spatial practices and for respatializing power. So perhaps the first element in creating this map is making the underlying epistemological assumptions visible and tracking that visibility throughout the life of the course. This requires making three inter-related moves. The first is to demystify and destabilize the old cartographic binaries set up by the academy and by the pedagogic and spatial practices within our syllabi so that we can think about the transnational, specifically transnational feminism, by looking at the ways cultural borders are crossed and the way hierarchies of place are normalized. The second attends to the hyperracialization and sexualization of the various "elsewheres." Precisely because the academy fetishizes these elsewheres in the service of its own identity formation, race and sex must be central to our thinking about the transnational. And the third would require that we ask very specifically what kinds of border crossings we want and what are their ethical dimensions? This is a tough question, for it has to do not necessarily with the question that there are, according to Richard Nagar, "varying forms of knowledge evolving in specific places," but, more crucially, "what we are in a position to do in producing knowledge, namely, constitute ourselves as political actors in institutions and processes both near and far" (2006: 154). Fundamentally, then, we are talking about breaking the "epistemological contract" (the term is Sylvia Wynter's [1995]) that consigns the hierarchy of space and posi-tions only those at the top as capable of producing and disseminating that knowledge. And breaking that epistemological contract would necessarily entail disinvesting these academic identities from the will to power, moving beyond a liberal "policy neutral" academic stance to actively developing a radical ethic that challenges power and global hegemonies.

This map requires that we take space and spatialization seriously. To think the transnational in relation to the inherited uneven geographies of place and space would require holding in tension questions of power, gender, race and space. Who resides where and what kinds of knowledges do these residencies generate? We would examine those oppositional spatial politics that are not in the first instance invested in reconstituting insides and outsides, the citizen and the noncitizen. The spatial links that the transnational makes visible need always to be emphasized so as not to reinscribe the normative cartographic rule of the transnational as elsewhere and therefore recycle colonial cartographies that support the mandate for conquest. It is these politics of spatialization, with their attendant ethical imperatives, that allow us to understand colonial/imperial racial and sexual underpinnings of border crossings "without losing ourselves" or privileging an elsewhere. Location matters in this model of a feminist solidarity transnationalism.[16] And we can learn how to be location specific without being location bound.

Based on this analysis then, our earlier definitions of the transnational in *Feminist Genealogies* would need to wrestle with the following: 1) the links between the politics of location, the spatiality of power and that of knowledge production; 2) the physicality and materiality of space in terms of contestation over land; 3) a sharper focus on the ethics of the cross-cultural production of knowledge; and 4) a foregrounding of questions of intersubjectivity, connectivity, collective responsibility and mutual accountability as fundamental markers of a radical praxis. Indeed it is the way we live our own lives as scholars, teachers and organizers, and our relations to labour and practices of consumption in an age of privatization and hegemonic imperial projects that are at stake here.

Clearly the world has undergone major seismic changes that have been difficult to imagine almost a decade ago. It may well be that the contradictions between the knowledges generated in the classroom and those generated within grassroots political mobilization have been more sharpened given the increased institutionalization of oppositional knowledges and the increased embeddedness of the academy within the imperial militaristic projects of the state. And yet it's clear to us that without our respective involvement in political work outside (and sometimes in the in-between spaces within) the academy, it would be almost impossible to navigate the still contested spaces we occupy within it, spaces where we are called upon to be consistently attentive to our spiritual and psychic health. And so we continue to do this work across the fictive boundaries of the academy, constantly wrestling with its costs, and knowing that the intellectual, spiritual and psychic stakes are high, but believing that it is imperative to engage in the struggles over the production of liberatory knowledges and subjectivities in the belly of the imperial beast.

Notes

1. Many thanks to Richa Nagar, Amanda Lock Swarr, Linda Peake, Jigna Desai, and Katherine McKitterick for invaluable feedback on this chapter. Many thanks to Jennifer Wingard for research assistance for this chapter.
2. We are now situated in academic contexts in the U.S. and Canada, although much of our work emerges from in our location in the U.S. academy for over two decades.
3. See especially Valentine Moghadam, *Globalizing Women* (2005). We should also note that the transnational is not always already a radical category or one that speaks to a transformative or liberatory praxis.
4. Witness the struggle of women of colour faculty denied tenure at the University of Michigan, Ann Arbor (Conference on Campus Lockdown: Women of Color Negotiating the Academic Industrial Complex, Ann Arbor, 15 April 2008) (Afrolez Production Blog 2008); witness also the struggle over the inclusion of "scholarship in action" as part of tenure and promotion guidelines at Syracuse

University (2007-2008) (Phelps 2007)

5. Silvia Federici and George Caffentzis, "CAFA and the 'Edu-Factory'," contribution to the edu-factory online discussion 5 June 2007, and "Rete per l'Autoformazione, Roma" edu-factory discussion, 11 March 2007. Chandra was part of the discussion in 2007. For more information contact <info@edu-factory.org>.

6. In this materialist reading we do not pose the question about whether the sacred cajoles us into thinking about space differently. To think about the sacred in relationship to space and to bending these cartographic rules, see McKittrick and Woods' (2007: 4) discussion of the Atlantic Ocean as a "geographic region that... represents the political histories of the disappeared," and at the same time a place of the unknowable. Coupling this tension between the "mapped" and the "unknown," they suggest that "places, experiences, histories, and people that 'no one knows' do exist, within our present geographic order."

7. See Chandra's earlier work (Mohanty 2003: chap. 7), where she argued for an anticapitalist feminist project that examines the political economy of higher education, defining the effects of globalization in the academy as a process that combines market ideology with a set of material practices drawn from the business world. See also Jacqui's examination of the curricular effects of academic downsizing, the failures of normative multiculturalism and liberal pluralism, and the critical imperatives we face at this moment to teach for justice (Alexander 2006: chaps. 3 and 4).

8. See, among others, Sunera Thobani (2007).

9. Most of the research for this essay was conducted in early 2006, and the syllabi we analyze were all accessed electronically. We deliberately chose not to use our own syllabi, or even to discuss the curricula at our own institutions.

10. This was true of all the syllabi, except for an introductory course to LGBTT/queer studies in which colonial, immigrant and native histories of queers of colour indicated a recognition of the transnational within the United States without identifying it as such (the terms used here were diaspora and globalization).

11. Often, globalization was used to signify the transnational, and sometimes the terms were used to signal the same phenomena.

12. See Alexander (2006: chap. 5) for a detailed discussion of cultural relativism in the context of the transnational feminist classroom.

13. See Alexander's chapter five, "Transnationalism, Sexuality, and the State: Modernity's Traditions at the Height of the Empire" (2006).

14. See "Diversity in Academe," The Chronicle of Higher Education, 26 September 2008, Section B; Smith (2005); Ward Churchill and Winona LaDuke (1992); Sarah Deer, "Federal Indian Law and Violent Crime," in Smith (2006: 32–41).

15. In Chandra's earlier work (2003: chap. 9) describing three pedagogical models used in "internationalizing" women's studies, she suggested that each of these perspectives was grounded in particular conceptions of the local and the global, of women's agency and of national identity, and that each curricular model mapped different stories and ways of crossing borders and building bridges. She also suggested that a "comparative feminist studies" or "feminist solidarity" model is the most useful and productive pedagogical strategy for feminist

cross-cultural work, claiming that it is this particular model that provides a way to theorize a complex relational understanding of experience, location and history such that feminist cross-cultural work moves through the specific context to construct a real notion of universal *and* of democratization rather than colonization. It is this model that can put into practice the idea of "common differences" as the basis for deeper solidarity across differences and unequal power relations.

16. We are indebted to Katherine McKittrick for this formulation.

References

Afrolez Productions Blog 2008 "Campus Lockdown: Women of Color Negotiating the Academic Industrial Complex" February 24 Afrolez Productions, http://www.afrolezproductions.com/blog/campus-lockdown-women-of-color-negotiating-the-academic-industrial-complex/

Alexander, M. Jacqui. 2006. *Pedagogies of Crossing: Meditations on Feminism, Sexual Politics, Memory, and the Sacred*. Durham: Duke University Press.

Alexander, M. Jacqui, and Chandra Talpade Mohanty. 1997. *Feminist Genealogies, Colonial Legacies, Democratic Futures*. New York: Routledge.

Bergeron, Suzanne. 2001. "Political Economy, Discourses of Globalization, and Feminist Politics." *Signs* 26(4): 983–1006.

Burman, Jenny. 2007. "Deportable or Admissible? Black Women and the Space of 'Removal'." In Katherine McKittrick and Clyde Woods (eds.), *Black Geographies and the Politics of Place*. Toronto: Between the Lines.

Churchill, Ward, and Winona LaDuke. 1992. "Native North America: The Political Economy of Radioactive Colonialism." In M. Annette James (ed.), *The State of Native America: Genocide, Colonization and Resistance*. Boston: South End Press.

Davies, Carole Boyce. 2007. "Towards African Diaspora Citizenship." In Katherine McKittrick and Clyde Woods (eds.), *Black Geographies and the Politics of Place*. Toronto: Between the Lines.

Deer, Sarah. 2006. "Federal Indian Law and Violent Crime." In Incite! Women of Color Against Violence (ed.), *Color of Violence: The Incite! Anthology*. Cambridge, MA: South End Press.

"Diversity in Academe." *The Chronicle of Higher Education*, 26 September 2008. Section B.

Federici, Silvia, and George Caffentzis. 2007. "CAFA and the 'Edu-Factory' First Round." Edufactory Web Journal, Sunday, 06 May. <http://www.edu-factory.org/edu15/index.php?option=com_content&view=article&id=106:cafa-and-the-edu-factory&catid=43:firstround>.

Feldman, Jonathan. 1989. *Universities in the Business of Repression: The Academic-Military-Industrial Complex in Central America*. Boston: South End Press.

LaDuke, Winona. 2005. *Recovering the Sacred: The Power of Naming and Reclaiming*. Toronto: Between the Lines.

Lawrence, Bonita, and Enakshi Dua. 2005. "Decolonizing Antiracism." *Social Justice* 21, 4: 120–38.

Mama, Amina. 2007. "Is It Ethical to Study Africa? Preliminary Thoughts on Scholarship and Freedom." *African Studies Review* 50,1: 1–26.

McKittrick, Katherine. 2006. *Demonic Grounds: Black Women and the Cartographies of Struggle*. Minneapolis: University of Minnesota Press.

McKittrick, Katherine, and Linda Peake. 2005. "What Difference Does Difference Make to Geography?" In Neil Castree, Ali Rogers and Douglas Sharman (eds.), *Questioning Geography*. Oxford: Blackwell.

McKittrick, Katherine, and Clyde Woods (eds.). 2007. *Black Geographies and the Politics of Place*. Toronto: Between the Lines.

Mindry, Deborah. 2001. "Nongovernmental Organizations, 'Grassroots' and the Politics of Virtue." *Signs* 26, 4: 1187–211.

Moghadam, V.M. 2005. *Globalizing Women: Transnational Feminist Networks*. Baltimore: Johns Hopkins University Press.

Mohanty, Chandra Talpade. 2003. *Feminism Without Borders: Decolonizing Theory, Practicing Solidarity*. Durham: Duke University Press.

Nagar, Richa. 2006. "Postscript: NGOs, Global Feminisms, and Collaborative Border Crossings." In Sangtin Writers and Richa Nagar (eds.), *Playing with Fire: Feminist Thought and Activism Through Seven Lives in India*. Minneapolis: University of Minneapolis Press.

Phelps, Louise Wetherbee. 2007. "Learning about Scholarship in Action in Concept and Practice." A White Paper From the Academic Affairs Committee of the University Senate, Syracuse University, Syracuse, New York.

Pinto, V. Oliveira. 2003. "The Lessons of Candomblé, The Lessons of Life." In M. Jacqui Alexander, Lisa Albrecht, Sharon Day and Mab Segrest (eds.), *Sing, Whisper, Shout, Pray! Feminist Visions for a Just World*. Fort Bragg: EdgeWork Books.

Radcliffe, Sarah A., Nina Laurie, and Robert Andolina. 2003. "The Transnationalization of Gender and Reimagining Andean Indigenous Development." *Signs* 29, 2: 387–416.

Rodriguez, Dylan. 2006. *Forced Passages: Imprisoned Radical Intellectuals and the U.S. Prison Regime*. Minneapolis: University of Minnesota Press.

Schaeffer-Gabriel, Felicity. 2006. "Planet-Love.com: Cyberbrides in the Americas and the Transnational Routes of U.S. Masculinity." *Signs* 31(2), 331-356.

Smith, Andrea. 2005. *Conquest: Sexual Violence and American Indian Genocide*. Cambridge, MA: South End Press.

___. 2006. "Heteropatriarchy and the Three Pillars of White Supremacy: Rethinking Women of Color Organizing." In Incite! Women of Color Against Violence (ed.), *Color of Violence: The Incite! Anthology*. Cambridge, MA: South End Press.

Sudbury, Julia (ed.). 2005. *Global Lockdown: Race, Gender, and the Prison-Industrial Complex*. New York: Routledge.

Thobani, Sunera. 2007. *Exalted Subjects: Subjects in the Making of Race and Nation in Canada*. Toronto: University of Toronto Press.

Wynter, Sylvia. 1995. "Breaking the Epistemological Contract on Black America." *Forum NHI* 2, 1: 41–57 and 64–70.

Chapter Three

SEXUAL DIVERSITY IN COSMOPOLITAN PERSPECTIVE

Elisabeth Young-Bruehl

The Globalization of Sexology and Changes in Its Categories

In the last decade or so, the concept of "sexual diversity" has shifted its meaning and compass in the Euro-American world, where the scientific study of sex — called sexology — began in earnest at the end of the nineteenth century. For most of the twentieth century, both lay people and scientists alike subscribed to a model of human sexuality stipulating that human sexuality normally (and normatively) has little diversity. There are just two sexes, male and female; two genders, masculine and feminine, with corollary social roles; and two kinds of sexual preference, same-sex and opposite-sex. "Sexual diversity" was roughly equivalent to "sexual pathology" and that meant (above all else) "non-heterosexual preference."

In the wake of the Euro-American second wave feminist movement and the gay liberation movement, the scientific study of sex became much more sophisticated and much less governed by prejudices against women and against homosexuals, so both the prejudices themselves and this Noah's Ark two-of-everything paradigm of sexuality could shift. Now, among progressive people around the world, homosexuality can be considered an ordinary, non-pathological type of sexuality; in the movement's political terms it is "different but equal." The political situation has changed so dramatically that a 2006 petition entitled "For the Universal Decriminalization of Homosexuality" was launched in hopes of getting the United Nations to favour abrogating the anti-gay laws of the seventy-five countries in the world where homosexuality is still a crime.

In the domain of the scientific study of sex, the result of the political shift and the paradigm shift has been that the biological sex binary of male and female has become a continuum that includes all kinds of intersex states between the extremes of male and female; the gender binary of masculine and feminine has turned into a "social construct" to be studied comparatively and deconstructed by sex activists, so that it, too, has become a continuum stretched between extremes of masculine and feminine gender identity and role; and bisexuality now encompasses heterosexuality and homosexuality as two extremes on its continuum (as Alfred Kinsey had proposed in the 1950s).

In the 1970s and 1980s much of the scientific impetus in the Euro-American world for the paradigm shift away from binarism and toward thinking in continua came from studies of gender identity and role, which revealed great diversity in womanhood and manhood around the world and across history, and which then helped medical practioners understand how to design flexible policies for addressing the HIV/AIDS pandemic. Recently impetus for the shift has come from the addition of "transpeople" to the list of people to be studied (and people doing the studying), for their experiences disturbed all of the taken for granted binaries at once. At the turn of the twenty-first century, sexual minorities were politically grouped as not just LGB but LBGT, Lesbian, Gay, Bisexual and Transgender.

But these very compactly stated scientific and political results, which I will explore further later, were also the consequence of a wave of new information about human sexuality that came to Euro-American researchers from researchers and political-sexual activists all over the world. As the Euro-American sexual liberation movements rippled outward, and then as local and international groups organized to combat the world-wide AIDS epidemic, sexual minorities that had been in hiding and often unnamed, unorganized, sequestered or persecuted "came out." With their visibility, a wealth of stories and data became available — and that meant, given the existence of new communications technologies, available around the world. To offer just one example, you can go to the Internet and find out from a newsgathering site like globalgayz.com that in 2003 Nepal's first ever organization for sexual minorities was founded, and that the Blue Diamond Society welcomed under its banner and to its AIDS-oriented medical clinics not just gay men, lesbians and transgender people but sex workers and people who engage in various types of ritual sexual practices from singing contests to transvestitism. Similar progressive political organizations in South Asia and elsewhere try not to be prescriptive about how people define themselves and are often critical of the Euro-American insistence on viewing a practice as defining an identity.

In terms of the amount of persecution suffered by sexual minorities, the globalization of the reformed scientific attention to prejudice and persecution and of the liberationist political struggle has had mixed results: in some areas, persecution has diminished, in others it has increased and become more public; in some areas, there is greater tolerance, in others greater backlash. For all kinds of sexual minorities, the recent rise of fundamentalisms in all the world's imperialistic religions, which has been intensified by globalization even in states with long secularizing trends, has been horrible. However, one trend is unambiguously progressive.

After 1989, when the human rights movement emerged from under the shadow of the Cold War, the struggle for civil rights conducted by the gay liberation movement in America and in most western European countries transformed into a worldwide struggle for human rights conducted by groups sharing experiences of persecution motivated by a wide range of prejudices, not just sexism and homophobia. The consolidation of the period of civil rights struggle and the commencement of the human rights struggle was signaled in 1990 when the World Health Organization removed homosexuality from its list of mental disorders and in 1991 when Amnesty International included persecution on grounds of sexual orientation in its reporting and then extended that inclusion to transpeople. The International Gay and Lesbian Human Rights Commission (IGLHRC) was founded in 1990 (and from the start it included transgender people's human rights in its mandate).

The Globalization of the Study of Prejudices Against Sexual Minorities and Sexuality

One of the great achievements of the recent study of sexuality has been to show that prejudice against either women or sexual minorities or both has always gone along with and promoted misinformation about sexuality. For example, when hormones were discovered in the 1920s, it was assumed that males had one kind of hormone —testosterone — and women another — estrogen — because men and women had to be very distinct beings, and no man should have any mixture of femaleness, which would make him homosexual. The extraordinary complexity of the human hormone system and the presence in all people of every type of hormone was slow to be appreciated — and still is full of mysteries. Misinformation, in turn, contributed to the petrification of the very prejudices that had produced it.

Historical and historiographical studies have freed contemporary scientists to look at human sexuality and the stories that have been told about it with much greater objectivity, and it has also provided the foundations for study of prejudice itself. After prejudice against women was clearly identified in the 1960s and given a name — sexism — that designated it as a prejudice, comparable to racism or anti-Semitism, that is, as involving characteristic acts and an ideology (not just the attitude long named misogyny), researchers could raise the question: Did this prejudice originate in a particular context or contexts, psychological and sociological? Is it now global or species-wide?

Once the question of sexism's origin had been raised and explored, it became obvious that the analogous question should be raised about homophobia, a prejudice which does not exist outside of contexts where sexism is endemic, as its forms — and they are plural — are all variants of sexism. Homophobia was named and understood as a prejudice in the 1970s, but to this day there is no word for prejudice against sexual minorities other than homosexuals, either generally or specifically, and it is not yet clearly understood that prejudices against sexual minorities other than homosexuals have been built up on the foundations of homophobias. Hermaphrodites (now more commonly known as intersexuals), for example, have in some times and places been persecuted, but there is no word in any language for such a prejudice. In some societies, transpeople — males living as females, or females living as males, who may or may not be anatomically intersexual or homosexual in terms of sexual practices — are held to be a third sex and valued, or at least not stigmatized. But in other societies, transpeople, particularly males living as females, are assumed (falsely) to be homosexual and are despised.

Sexual minorities persecuted from nameless motivation obviously have in common that they challenge sex and gender binarism conventions or stereotypes; they are non-conforming in the matters of either genital appearance or gender role or both, and they may also be non-conforming in the matter of sexual preference (as they are assumed to be). Diverse sexual minorities have become hated in contexts where conformism itself has become valued as the means for group cohesion. And a comparative historical survey can indicate, further, I believe, that the most prejudicial environments are generated when groups that have achieved group cohesion defensively, while fending off persecution and humiliation, then turn aggressive and use their group cohesion for conquest, or some form of imperialism.

To use psychoanalytic terms for this aggressively maintained group cohesion, persecuted groups master their group trauma with conquest over other groups. Prejudice against sexual minorities, including homosexuals, seems strongest in groups that have achieved cohesion defensively through an ideology of active, self-punishing asceticism or body rejection. In persecuted, defended groups, sexual minorities are accused of being the reason for the group's weakness, or of being a threat to the reproductive strength that might overcome weakness, or of interfering with a vision of how to transcend persecution by asceticism in this world and by focus on life in the next world. As such groups turn aggressive themselves, seeking the this-worldly power they have been denied, they accuse their sexual minorities of being like the outsiders who are to be conquered. The hated sexual minorities are usually said to inhibit or undermine (as a kind of fifth column) the conquest project by not contributing to the regular reproduction that would reinforce the group's imperial strength.

Within some persecuted groups that subscribe to an ascetic ideology, sexual minorities are felt to challenge by their very existence, which calls attention to sexuality and to the body. The most influential example of this sort of ideological asceticism in world history has been the small, persecuted eastern Mediterranean Christian communities of the first century after Christ, in which anticipation of the next life and denigration of life in this world (along with apocalyptic visions of the imminent end of this world) became the norm. At the same moment in the first century, there was an ascetic strain in persecuted Jewish communities, but it was less strong and less otherworldly among the Jews, who emphasized family bonds and regular reproduction to provide for group survival. The third Abrahamic religion, Mohammedanism, the least persecuted in its originary moment, was not body-rejecting or anti-sexual or otherworldly, and it was also, of the three religions, the least intolerant of sexual minorities.

Early in the first century, St. Paul, echoing contemporary neo-Platonic and Jewish ascetic writings, railed against both male homosexuality and cross-dressing (or what would now be called male-to-female transgender behavior). The most consistently despised practice was sodomy, named (as it was in Jewish and Islamic traditions as well) after the biblical story of Sodom and Gomorrah, which had been interpreted —contemporary scholars would say grossly misinterpreted — as a story of male homosexual activity punished directly by God.

From its imperial inception in 313 A.D., the Christian Empire proclaimed by the Roman Constantine, drawing on its heritage of body rejection or anti-sexuality or asceticism, and perpetuating that heritage through an ascetic priesthood in its Catholic branch, has been the greatest single source in world history of prejudice against male homosexuals, male-to-female transpeople, and male transvestites. Peoples who came under its expanding sway, as did the Gothic or Visgothic peoples who vanquished the Romans, adopted its edicts. As a general rule, it can be said that the more militantly proselytizing the Christians have been, the more they have engaged in repression of male deviants — and eventually female as well, although because female homosexuality does not directly threaten patrilineal reproduction it is less politically offensive.

Among the diverse Muslim societies that were suppressed by the Christian crusaders, homosexuality had generally been condemned, with reference both to the Qu'ran, where the "people of Lot" are censured, and to the Haditha (sayings attributed to Mohammed). But at the same time, the "Greek love" of older men for their beautiful protégés and courtiers was the subject of a revered genre of Arabic love poetry and homosexuality between males was, in reality, punished only if it had been witnessed or was in some way publicly expressed. Tolerance for private acts was much greater than in the early Christian and Jewish traditions, and this was especially the case through the great seventh and eighth century period of Muslim rule in the Iberian peninsula, when the Umayyad Muslims subdued the debased Visgothic culture, but then ruled peacefully from their capital in Cordoba, encouraging Muslim, Christian and Jewish peoples of Andalusia to intermarry freely.

In the modern Muslim world, militant prejudice against homosexuals and other sexual minorities has gone along with militant nationalism, which can be described as the effort of diverse types of Muslims to recover from their humiliating suppression by the Christian Empire, which started in the period of the Crusades. Among modern capitalistic Christian imperialists, the British, whose educational institutions were single-sex and quite puritanical, excelled at sexual suppression, particularly of their common practice, sodomy. As in the early Christian communities, an ascetic form of Islam emerged during the rise of persecuting capitalist imperialism as the form most intolerant of sexual minorities, and Wahabbism retains that distinction to this day, when it has grown progressively more imperialistic.

Recently — although the number of Muslim nations in which homosexuality is punishable with death was reduced from seven to five as the Taliban was defeated in Afghanistan and as Saddam Hussein was overthrown in Iraq — Saudi Arabia, the chief seat of Wahabbism, has grown less and less tolerant and Wahabbism has been exported from it into terrorist camps across the Middle East. The 1979 ascetic fundamentalist revolution in Iran brought about an enormous wave of sexual persecution — for homosexuality, but also for adultery — that has also been exemplary for fundamentalists in other Muslim nations where homosexuality is said to be a Western aberration, an import. The importation charge is also made in many African nations, Muslim and non-Muslim, where dictatorial leaders claim that their sexual minorities are products of Western influence and that there is no such things as indigenous African homosexuality or transgenderism.

The Christian Empire's anti-minority prejudices are the world's most potent example of prejudices that began in ascetic social practices turning aggressive and, in the context of developing imperialism, becoming more political — that is, becoming like planks in party platforms. The contrast between the Christian Empire's anti-sexual minority prejudices and the situations in parts of the world uninfluenced by it — or by Christian-influenced Islam — is very stark. In ancient China, for example, during periods of both Taoist and Confucian religious practice, male homosexuality was common in the courts of the emperors. No anti-homosexual legislation was created in China until Christian missionaries brought along their models, although by far the worst period of persecution was during nationalist upsurge of the Chinese Cultural Revolution led by Mao, which was a period of assault upon the corrupting Westernization of China.

Tolerance for Multisexuality in the Globalizing World

Recent scientific study of sex, more aware of this history of prejudice and reducing the amount of misinformation it has generated, has established that the human species — like all the mammalian species — has evolved as a species in which there is great diversity of sexual constitution and behavior (with behavior not in any simple way the consequence of constitution or in any simple way correlated to gender). That is, it became obvious that human sexuality is very diverse in constitution and expression when it was understood that all human beings are mixtures of chromosomal sex (the presence or absence of X and Y chromosomes), hormonal sex (involving a mixture of many types of hormones), gonadal sex (the presence or absence of testes and ovaries), external genitals and reproductive sexual functions (involving the capacity to produce ova and lactate or to produce sperm). Hermaphroditism (now usually called intersexuality), originally referenced exclusively to the appearance of a person's genitals, is now known to be quite common and to come in varying degrees, involving different configurations of chromosomes, hormones, gonads and genitals. Approximately seventy intersex syndromes have been described. There are more than twenty-four known causes for genital ambiguity alone and worldwide as many as 2 percent to 4 percent of newborns have ambiguous genitals, while many more are intersexual in ways that cannot be detected visually.

There are places in the contemporary world where certain intersex conditions are acknowledged without stigmatization. Similarly, there are societies where transgender people are not stigmatized — indeed, where they are elevated. Among many Native Americans tribes, *nadles* or "Two-Spirit People," constituting a third sex and often entering into same-sex marriages, are honored with a special status and specific tasks, including skill transmission and wisdom teaching. What is known in sexology as sexual identity is not assumed by many Native Americans to be a developmental product, a conjunction of many factors, biological and psychological, which a person claims as an identity. Rather, sexual role or performance is a product of shamanistic dreaming; it is assigned by a dream and the dreamer chooses to welcome the assignment as a gift, a vocation.

In other traditions as well sexuality is thought to be produced by choice of practice or choice of way of being sexual, not just by inborn makeup. Sexual identity is not a distinct kind of identity, but part of the microcosm that each individual is. In the ancient Taoist sexual theory, all people were thought to be born with a mixture of the cosmic male bodyspirit yang and the female bodyspirit ying, which are exchanged by adults in sexual intercourse. Right sexual practice was supposed to preserve a person's unique harmonious bodyspirit mixture, so men, for example, were cautioned against exclusive homosexual practice because it involved too much yang-yang mixing and would result in not enough ying. Bisexual practice not only served reproduction, but also served yang-ying calibration, keeping males female enough for harmony. By contrast, in cultures like the ancient Greek or the modern Melanesian, male characteristics were thought to be enhanced by transmission of semen from an older man to a younger, so homosexual practice was key to initiation rites or rites of manhood that are meant to keep a boy from being too female or too much of the female world of his mother.

Considering these diverse philosophies and practices, it seems to me generally accurate to say that, as defensive asceticism is the taproot of prejudice against sexual diversity, the taproot of tolerance for it or appreciation of it is a sense that sexuality is a manifestation of a bodyspirit harmony (that is, a bisexual or ambisexual or omnisexual harmony) and that how this harmony is manifested is a matter of choice or practice. To say the same thing psychodynamically, tolerance or appreciation involves not splitting (or, in theoretical terms, not embracing binarism). Not-split persons are ones who have integrated what is felt to be male/masculine and what is felt to be female/feminine in their makeup. (Among Christian fundamentalists today, "conversion therapy" is promoted for treating homosexuals, and what this means is that homosexuals who cannot split off their forbidden desire and turn into heterosexuals must become ascetic to avoid sinning. Splitting is required, instituted, in either solution.)

Combining these two generalizations, it can be said that defensive asceticism is an extreme form of splitting; that is, so drastically are masculine and feminine split (or purified into extremes) that both disappear, both become disembodied. In the Abrahamic monotheistic traditions, worship is focused on a disembodied male deity who may be accompanied by some form of Holy Spirit that retains the last vestiges of a female component without being available for reproduction in a heterosexual manner. Ascetic splitting itself is revered. By contrast, polytheistic traditions generally include in their pantheons at least a few gods who are hermaphroditic or homosexual or transgendered in some form, that is, they represent the diversity characteristic of human families or social groups. Not-splitting is revered. Within polytheistic societies — the Hindu societies of India, for example — the kind of prejudice characteristic of monothesism only appeared under colonial conditions. In Nepal — to go back to an earlier example — the ancient Hindu and Buddhist temple art depicts many sexual practices and behaviors that were forbidden under British rule.

Sexual Pathology in Global Context

Scientific study of sexual behavior in the Euro-American world was for so long dominated by categories of normality and deviance in relation to the binaries male/female, masculine/feminine and same sex/opposite sex preference, that all kinds of sexual pathology were fitted to that paradigm. Any pathologies that did not fit into the binary paradigm were almost completely unstudied (although not undocumented). The psychological concept of perversion and the sociological category sex offender, for example, were both organized by the assumption that homosexuality is the key perversion and the related assumption that most sex offenders are homosexual. All other perversions were described in relation to homosexuality, and study of sex offenders hardly existed outside of forensics, where offenders were understood as homosexual, which meant, for example, that heterosexual sex offenders in domestic situations (wife batterers) or men ordered or permitted to commit rape as part of military campaigns were not identified as sex offenders.

One of the most important consequences of the paradigm shift away from binary thinking and toward thinking in terms of continua of sex, gender and preference experiences, has been the opportunity the shift has presented to reconsider sex pathology — a reconsideration that is in course around the world. To put this reconsideration in a nutshell: after both the phenomenon of sexual abuse of women and the phenomenon of child abuse and neglect became subjects for scientific study in the 1960s — and the links between these phenomena emerged — pathology was no longer thought of so much in terms of sexual diversity or deviancy as in terms of abusiveness. That is, the focus is now on the quality of the relationship existing between persons engaging in sexual behaviors.

To my mind, this refocus should result in a redefinition of sex pathology as sexual behavior, usually manifesting a specific ideology and certainly involving characteristic acts, which is non-relational (or relationship-denying). Non-relational, as I am using it, means that the pathological person cannot treat another involved in his or her act as a person, an equal — or, one would say in political terms, as a human with human rights. The person's practices involve some form of ownership and do not involve consent or respect for the other's wishes. To use a term from the history of marriage, there is nothing companionate in a sex offender's sexual relationships — or non-relationships. By this non-relational definition of perversion, homosexuality is obviously not a perversion, as it does not involve reducing a person to less than a person or denying human rights (no more than do heterosexuality or bisexuality). A transgender person is just as capable of a respectful, equal relationship as a non-transgender person.

In the world today, even though there has been progress in writing international conventions to articulate and secure human rights generally and the rights of women and children specifically (if not yet of sexual minorities), a documentable increase is occurring in perverse sexual behaviors (thus defined). This is being fueled by globalizing social and technological conditions that foster abuse of women and children, which, although such abuses are as old as patriarchy, now have novel features. For example, most of the world's wars since 1989 have been interstate wars, and in these wars rape and child rape have come to be used instrumentally to disrupt reproduction within an enemy ethnic group contending for control of the state. An estimated 500,000 women and girls were raped during the Rawandan genocide (Peacewoman 2011).

The most obvious abuse type with novel features is child pornography, which can now be manufactured easily and inexpensively with digital cameras and disseminated on the Internet by individuals, without the kinds of networks and organizations once required. Solicitation of sex with minors and marketing of child prostitution, too, have moved onto the Internet, although trafficking women and children for prostitution still requires the smuggling and brothels long familiar to police. The rise in recent years of global trade has been accompanied by an increase in the transportation of women and children around the world for both labor and sex work; unemployment rate increases in both developed and undeveloped countries have also contributed to increases of sexual trafficking, sexual violence and sexually transmitted disease. Similarly, as the number of war zones (especially intrastate ones) in the world has risen, so have the number of refugees and people without a safe home, and the consequences of this for abuse of women and children are obvious.

For many years, research into sexual abuse of women and children was hampered by lack of agreed upon definitions and differences in definitions across states and cultures; by lack of mandatory reporting and inconsistency in reporting; and by the prejudice, which I mentioned before, about the perpetrators being deviants in the now out-dated terms. Pedophilia was widely assumed to be a subspecies of homosexuality, although it is now obvious — in various cultural contexts — that the vast majority of pedophiles are heterosexual males who chose their victims, whether male or female, because of their non-adult status and the quality of their vulnerability or powerlessness, not just because of their male or female sexual characteristics. A pedophile can avoid humiliation in adult relationships — including with adults who do not want to be infantilized — and play out sexual fantasies of various types with little resistance from an uncomprehending child.

Nowhere in the world is there a concept for a prejudice, comparable to sexism, directed against children — no childism. However, in the eighteenth century the word "misopedia" (child hatred) was coined to acknowledge child hatred as comparable to misogyny and misandry. In the Century of the Child, as the twentieth century was hopefully named by late nineteenth century child protectionists and opponents of child labor, child hatred was to be eliminated. But we who, despite considerable reform and even the emergence of societies characterizing themselves as "child-centered," live with the obvious fact that child hatred did not recede, still do not speak of a childist culture when considering a culture that promotes or sanctions any form of child abuse and neglect. We do not speak of groups that are childist, as child pornographers are, or child sex traffickers, or armies recruiting child soldiers.

Hopefully, as sexual minorities whose behaviors are "different but equal" come to consume less and less of the attention of both students of sexuality and people prejudiced against sexuality and sexual variation, the really problematic sexual minority — those whose sexual behaviors are abusive — will be better understood and the human rights of their victims more understandingly and effectively protected.

References

Abelove, H., and Michèle Aina Barale (eds.). 1993. *The Lesbian and Gay Studies Reader* New York: Routledge

Altman, Dennis. 2001. *Global Sex*. Chicago: University of Chicago

Baird, Vanessa. 2001. *No-Nonsense Guide to Sexual Diversity*. Toronto: New Internationalist Press.

Halperin, David. 2001. *How To Do The History of Homosexuality* Chicago: University of Chicago Press

Lacquer, Thomas. 1990. *Making Sex*. Cambridge, MA: Harvard University Press.

Lancaster, R., and M. Di Leonardo (eds.). 1997. *The Gender/Sexuality Reader*. New York: Routledge.

Nagel, Joan. 2003. *Race, Ethnicity, and Sexuality Intimate Intersections, Forbidden Frontiers*. Berekley: University of California Press.

Parke, Richard, and John Gagnon. 1995. *Conceiving Sexuality; Approaches to Sex Research in a Post-Modern World*. New York: Routledge.

<Peacewomen.org>. Women's International League for Peace and Freedom. 2011. *Rwanda: The Word on Women — No Progress without Women: Rwanda's Journey to Complete the Millennium Development Goals* <http://www.peacewomen.org/news_article.php?id=3958&type=news>.

Preves, Sharon. 2003. *Intersex and Identity*. New Brunswick, NJ: Rutgers University Press

Richardson, D., and S. Seidman (eds.). 2002. *Handbook of Lesbian & Gay Studies*. Thousand Oaks, CA: Sage

Stein, Arlene. 1997. *Sex and Sensibility*. Berekely: University of California Press.

Websites

Global Gayz <www.globalgayz.com>.

The International Gay and Lesbian Human Rights Commission <www.iglhrc.org/>.

Part Two

FEMINISM AND THE ACADEMY: (RE)ENGAGING THE "KNOWLEDGE REVOLUTION"

Chapter Four

UNIVERSITIES UPSIDE DOWN
The Impact of the New Knowledge Economy

Margaret Thornton

Transforming the Academy

A large advertisement in an Australian newspaper caught my eye in late 2008. It was headed, "Entire University Campus for Lease: QUT Carseldine Campus, Queensland" (*Financial Review* 2008: 36). The fully equipped campus property of 45ha was described as a desirable piece of real estate that was available for up to twenty-five years. However, what was not mentioned was of more interest to me. This was that the campus, which had formerly housed the Queensland University of Technology's Faculty of Arts, was closed down in July 2008 following a decision by university management. I had been a speaker at the Faculty's "Last Post" colloquium in late 2007 when it was hoped that a change of federal government might win a reprieve, but this was not to be. The campus was abandoned and had still not found a tenant by late 2010.

To replace the Faculty of Arts, the university established a new Creative Industries Faculty. "Creative industries," a phrase of the twenty-first century, has been described by Yarrow (2010, emphasis in original) as a "weaselly worded, neo-liberal concept," which "usually involves obliterating *unproductive* spaces or communities, and developing them into revitalized and funky places" (see also Lovink and Rossiter 2007). Now there is nothing wrong with creative industries per se, which include visual and performing arts, the entertainment industry and technical production, but where was the space to study the liberal arts — history, philosophy, classics, feminist or Indigenous studies? There was none, leading Guille (2008) to liken QUT to a technical college. In the new faculty, it was clearly creative entrepreneurialism that counted, which would be effected through liaisons with business. The fate of QUT's Faculty of Arts in a neoliberal context is a graphic illustration of my thesis.

For centuries, the university has been viewed as the custodian of culture, the seat of higher learning and the paradigmatic site of free enquiry. These lofty aims have been turned upside down by a constellation of values emanating from the interstices of neoliberalism, the new knowledge economy and globalization. The result is that the university as a key knowledge producer is now primarily regarded as a source of wealth creation to be exploited. As the market enters the soul of the university, it has caused the commitment to traditional values to contract.

The transformation occurred within a context of a notable swing to the right in global politics. Whereas social liberalism paid at least a modicum of attention to the idea of the public good, equality and distributive justice, neoliberalism shifted the focus from civil society to the market, with a correlative fixation on the interests of the individual and the accumulation of private wealth. To this extent, neoliberalism has revived some of the tenets of classical liberalism, although it endorses a more positive conception of state power (Olssen and Peters 2005: 315). It might be noted that Hayek, described as the father of neoliberalism, emphasized the importance of knowledge as the key to economic growth in the 1930s and 1940s (1937, 1945), but it has taken the technological revolution for the significance of knowledge as a commodity to be realized. Lyotard (1984) percipiently observed almost three decades ago that knowledge had replaced land, raw materials and cheap labour in the struggle for power among nation states. The new knowledge economy nevertheless engenders risks that perpetually "haunt" entrepreneurialism in ways not previously known (Kenway et al. 2006; Beck 1992), as the recent global financial crisis has reminded us. To abate the risk, it is believed that new knowledge must possess use value in the market.

In this chapter,[1] I consider three significant phases in the history of the university from a feminist perspective: modernization, feminization and corporatization. I begin by overviewing the trajectory of change from the emergence of the modern university and the contestation over the claim to the universality of knowledge by feminist scholars. As a touchstone in this respect, I will have recourse to the Canadian Research Institute for the Advancement of Women publication of 1984, *Knowledge Reconsidered: A Feminist Overview*. I then consider the paradigm shift in the academy arising from the emergence of the new knowledge economy and its ramifications for feminist knowledge. In conclusion, I suggest that the new knowledge economy has facilitated the remasculinization of the academy behind a façade of rationality, neutrality and technocratic knowledge.

The Idea of the University

The inception of the modern university is marked by Von Humboldt's establishment of the University of Berlin in 1810. The modern university was concerned with the erudition, learning and refinement of the emerging bourgeoisie rather than mediaeval scholasticism or aristocratic *noblesse oblige*. Bourgeois revolutionary education was rational, universal, secular and enlightened (Miyoshi 2002: 52), values that came to represent the essence of a liberal university education.

John Henry Newman (1976) eloquently captures *the idea* of the university, the passing of which many rue (for example, Rowland 2008) even though Newman's famous treatise is directed towards the education of Irish Catholic gentlemen. The kernel of the idea was that the university constituted a site of free inquiry — hence its liberal descriptor. Thus, according to Newman, the university was not constrained by particular presuppositions, vocationalism or practical skills. Even within a religious context, Newman considered the role of the university to be intellectual rather than moral. Most significantly, knowledge should be pursued for its own sake, not for instrumental reasons. Thus, the end of knowledge was knowledge itself. Newman (1976: 96) identified the attributes of liberal education as: "freedom, equitableness, calmness, moderation, and wisdom." Academic freedom as articulated by Newman was to become the leitmotif of the liberal incarnation of the university, which, at least in the abstract, allowed a thousand flowers to bloom.

While knowledge for its own sake has connotations of the ivory tower that serves no functional purpose, the crucial role of the modern university in preserving the culture of the nation state revealed that it in fact served several functions. First of all, the liberal ideal was a political tool for the creation of good liberal citizens, particularly in the United States (Ryan 1998: 95). The study of the humanities and the natural sciences was believed to fashion character, although I reiterate that it was generally only the character of upper class and bourgeois men deemed to be of concern. Indeed, the elitism of the university was effectively deployed in the nineteenth century to exclude women and racialized Others, as well as to suppress democratic moves by the working class. Overseas, this cultural elitism was invoked by European nations to promote notions of superiority over colonized peoples. Hence, the university supported imperialism and global capitalism, as well as nationalism. Other instances of instrumentality are also discernible, such as the centrality of basic and applied science to the German university from the second half of the nineteenth century. Humboldt, unlike Newman, believed in the linkage of teaching and research in the modern university. The nexus between the national defence system and the American university in the mid-twentieth century underscores the importance of the applied research model (Delanty 2002: 37), which was to become the linchpin of academic capitalism.

Nostalgia for an idealized notion of the university in an age of overt functionality should not cause us to lose sight of the reality. The assumption that the university as a site of liberal education was formerly class-free, unrestricted, self-motivated and unbiased is a persistent myth (Myoshi 2002: 53). Indeed, first wave feminists agitated to be let into this masculinist world, inspired by the idealized vision of universality, neutrality and objectivity. The emancipist focus was directed towards treating women as rational and fully human (Fitzgerald 1996: 39).

Knowledge Reconsidered

By the late twentieth century, feminist acceptance of the claim to the universality of knowledge had lost some of its allure. Second wave feminists were no longer content with merely being "let into" the academy as it was, but sought to transform the nature of knowledge and the structures of power. The knowledge that had been assiduously safeguarded throughout the western intellectual tradition and transmitted in the belief that it was objective, neutral and true began to be dissected and exposed by feminist scholars as subjective and biased.

The feminist critique challenged the very presuppositions that had sustained the western intellectual tradition. This is despite the fact that the interrogation of known knowledge underpins the notion of free inquiry central to the liberal university (Axelrod et al. 2001: 52). Unsurprisingly, what was perceived to be an epistemological assault on foundational knowledge was highly contentious. There was clearly a limit to critical thinking, which included challenging the dominant tradition of moral philosophy and culture that instructed women to be silent in the presence of men (Keohane 1983: 92). This dictum resulted in not just the devaluation of women's voices and ideas but also the difficulty of accepting women as authoritative knowers. The new feminist knowledge signalled a paradigm shift in the academic social order.

Across the disciplines, feminist scholars systematically revealed how the denigration of women's activities operated to augment male power and cohesion (Epstein 1983: 151). Despite the resentment and antipathy, the new forms of knowledge gradually began to influence what is known and what is knowable (Langland and Gove 1983: 2), although masculinist sceptics remained unconvinced. The work of Canadian feminist theorists, the sociologist, Dorothy Smith (1988, 1990), and the philosopher, Lorraine Code (1991), were influential in developing new understandings of knowledge that drew on feminist subjectivities. The interdisciplinarity of women's studies was also a crucial aspect of the distinctiveness of feminist knowledge.

Nevertheless, any notion that the new discourse of women's studies denoted a universal "woman" was soon scuttled. "She" was criticized for the insularity of her white, middle class orientation. She lost her credibility because Indigenous women, non-English speaking background women, lesbians, women with disabilities and poor women felt marginalized. The implosion of the category woman coincided with the postmodern turn. French theorists, such as Foucault, Derrida, Lyotard and Lacan, all similarly challenged the notions of universality and truth that had for so long been associated with the idea of the university. The ensuing culture wars highlighted the contestation over the authority of the incumbents and their right to map out and safeguard the territory vis-à-vis the new feminist, postmodern and cultural theory contenders.

The gatekeepers, however, claimed that the challengers lacked rigour and were "too political." They had an ideological standpoint, unlike the Benchmark Men of the academy who were presumably perched on an Archimedean pinpoint that arose from their claim to universality and neutrality. The courses of the newcomers were denigrated, closed down or rendered anodyne and less threatening. In many institutions, women's studies disappeared in favour of more acceptable, de-gendered nomenclatures, such as diversity or gender studies.

Were these attacks crude manifestations of the backlash and ploys to safeguard the preserve of Benchmark Men, or did they represent a new epistemic moment that signalled a shift away from the category woman? While "she" had served a useful political and legal purpose, was she now past her prime? Did the widespread disappointment in her also herald the shift away from one-dimensionality in favour of interrogating masculinity, as well as Indigeneity, sexuality and postcoloniality? While some feminist scholars embraced postmodernism, acknowledging the one-dimensionality of the universal woman, others felt that the postmodern attack was a manifestation of the backlash that emerged just when women began speaking up for themselves (Nicholson 1995: 80). It is difficult to disentangle these elements of backlash that seem to be a perennial counterpoint to women's struggle for acceptance within the academy.

Despite the crisis of legitimation that postmodernism highlighted, a tsunami of greater magnitude was about to envelope the university and change it irretrievably. Its potential for harm was also commensurably far greater and, as I will argue, more insidious.

Knowledge Capitalism

What may be termed the third revolutionary phase in the recent history of the university, after modernization and feminization, is that of corporatization, emanating from the new knowledge economy. This phase has produced a string of new terms that only a short while ago would have been viewed as dissonant and disjunctive, such as "academic capitalism" (Slaughter and Leslie 1997) and "the enterprise university" (Marginson and Considine 2000). Regardless of the descriptor, the reality is that the university is now the preeminent site of knowledge production deployed by contemporary nation states to generate wealth.

Burton-Jones (1999: 3) suggests that the change in favour of the new knowledge economy is as profound as the industrial revolution. He explains that new knowledge is a form of capitalism with the same distinctive features:

> Capitalism as we know it, and emerging Knowledge Capitalism, both thrive on capital accumulation, open market competition, free trade, the power of the individual, and the survival of the fittest. (Burton-Jones 1999: 20)[2]

All capitalist economies now wish to exploit knowledge as an untapped source of wealth. The phenomenon has gathered momentum all over the world, not just in the West but also in China and Eastern Europe. Indeed, it is notable that nation states seeking to enhance their standing as new knowledge economies have the support of significant international bodies — the OECD (Kahim and Foray 2006), the IMF[3] and the World Bank (1994, 2007) — which are concerned to maximize productivity by fostering scientific and technological innovation (Johnstone et al 1998). The global spread of the logic of the market renders effective resistance virtually impossible.

"New knowledge" is not knowledge in the sense of the accumulated fruit of wisdom referred to by Newman or that associated with the transformative power of feminist knowledge envisaged by the authors of *Knowledge Reconsidered*. New knowledge is a term of art that refers to useful knowledge (know-how as opposed to know-what), which may be utilized to impart vocational skills to future new knowledge workers as well as to generate wealth. The notion of applied knowledge captures the slippage between "knowledge" and "information" that has occurred. The philosophical conditions for knowledge as traditionally understood — belief, truth and justification — are not satisfied by information, which is defined as "data transmitted from a 'sender' to a 'receiver'" (Peters 2002: 27). Perhaps the most significant manifestation of the dystopian effect of the knowledge society is that knowledge is no longer viewed as wisdom but data (Nowotny et al 2001: 12). Instead of the intellectual passion for ideas associated with scholastic and Enlightenment knowledge, there is now what has been described by Dominique Foray (2006: 13) as a "wild passion for private property in the realm of knowledge creation." This has contributed to the way in which bureaucratic and market discourse invariably trumps academic discourse. Readings' (1996: 21–43) discussion of the construction of "excellence" as a vacuous marketing tool illustrates the point.

The introduction of business principles into the university is not an altogether new phenomenon, however. The influential American theorist, Thorstein Veblen, who, like Newman, believed that the university was for the pursuit of knowledge for its own sake, identified the deleterious effects of business on universities a century ago (1954: 135). Selling intellectually impoverished courses for profit is also not new (Noble: 2001). Nevertheless, the new managerialism that is orchestrated by a nation state (for example, Department for Education and Skills, U.K.: 2003), or group of states,[4] is infinitely more far-reaching in its endeavours to deploy the new knowledge produced by universities for profit. Despite its potentially devastating effects for the future of the academy, the transformation of the university has been accepted with remarkable alacrity by faculty, students and society at large (Myoshi 2002: 52), which has enabled the academic capitalist discourse to be normalized. The evisceration of academic authority in favour of top-down managerial power, underpinned by manifold technologies of audit, has ensured that academics have quickly learned to adapt to the new environment. In fact, this third paradigm shift attests to the effectiveness of managerial compliance mechanisms that have largely displaced academic debate (Rowland 2006: 14).

In the twenty-first century, the public university is no longer certain what it is for as its orientation shifts from civil society to the market. Those parts of the university unable to demonstrate profitability face an uncertain future as indicated at the outset with the example of QUT's Arts Faculty. A similar pressure is confronting humanities and social sciences faculties elsewhere. Universities are beset with an anxiety to disprove any suggestion of uselessness. A British Academy report, for example, recently set out to prove that the humanities and social sciences were functional in terms of wealth generation, as well as public policy, health and well-being, and business (British Academy 2008; LSE Public Policy Group 2008). Even the United States, where higher education is diverse compared with other countries, has been profoundly affected by the intensity of change (Newman et al. 2004). Teaching and research have both been transformed by this academic capitalist environment, but in distinctive ways.

Teaching: Students as Consumers

Massification and privatization can be identified as the twin characteristics of the education revolution at a time when the neoliberal state has retreated from its responsibility for funding public universities. The shift from elite to mass was symbolically effected in Australia in 1988 and in the United Kingdom in 1990 by converting colleges of advanced education and polytechnics respectively into universities overnight. The vastly increased number of students attending the new universities were not expected to be the beneficiaries of a liberal university education — for its own sake — but to be trained as productive workers who would augment the new knowledge economy. In fact, they would be more likely to have their horizons narrowed rather than broadened by their university experience in order to fit them for the world of productive work. This phenomenon, which is by no means restricted to new universities, is aptly described by Bousfield as "vocationalising the curriculum" (Bousfield 1996: 72). It is distinguishable from embarking upon a specific vocational specialization, such as law. The effect of vocationalism has been to skew courses across the entire spectrum of the university towards applied fields and the acquisition of skills.

The trend towards privatization of so-called public universities emerges from treating education as a commodity. Again, Australia is a dramatic example, as free higher education was an initiative of the Whitlam Government in 1974, but it is now a case of user-pays as elsewhere. As fees are ratcheted up and students assume responsibility for more and more of the cost of their education, they have assumed all the characteristics of consumers purchasing a product, while academics have been relegated to the category of "service providers." As market players, universities must concentrate on satisfying the demands of the student body, not only to maximize university income, but also to attract the best students in order to increase their market share vis-à-vis competitors.

The transformation of students into consumers has inevitably contributed to the subversion of university ideals, for they are more likely to be interested in credentialism than the pursuit of a liberal education. Having one eye to ballooning education debt and one eye to an assured career path in an uncertain world has reified the swing towards vocationalism. Commodification has encouraged a dilution or a sloughing off of the liberal curriculum altogether, a phenomenon that is notable in the case of law, where the focus is on preparing students for the corporate track (for example, Arthurs 1998; Thornton 2007). Regardless of discipline, the emphasis is now on marketable skills, which encourage a less reflexive, theoretical and critical approach to the knowledge transmitted. Instrumentalism also encourages a pedagogy that is aptly captured by Freire's banking metaphor (1996: 53–57). The skills/applied focus is designed to appeal to prospective employers, thereby strengthening the idea of a conveyor belt between universities, corporate law firms and business.

The shift to a user-pays model has also contributed to a resiling from the humanities and liberal arts in favour of business. Ryan observes that in the U.S., where the neoliberal swing occurred earlier than elsewhere, BAs in Arts and Sciences decreased from 46 to 26 percent between 1968 and 1986, whereas business degrees, formerly only one-third as numerous as degrees in Arts and Sciences, are now equally as numerous (Ryan 1998: 148). A study of the Australian undergraduate enrolment data found that while there was an overall increase of 36 percent in the decade 1994–2004, the proportion of students enrolled in Management and Commerce increased by 70 percent (Krause et al. 2005: 80). Of course, business does not have to be taught in an applied way; it can include critical, prudential and ethical dimensions but, as already pointed out, commodification tends to promote a facilitative or "how-to" approach at the expense of critique.

Not only are business courses the most popular in the contemporary vocational university, but higher education itself has become a business or an industry, signifying its changed conceptualization in terms of the market. In Australia, higher education surpassed tourism in 2007 as the third biggest export earner after coal and iron. Once again, it is business, which embodies the international language of communication, that is most sought after by international students. The new knowledge economy has become essential to nation states, which means that states themselves have a vested interest in a regime that privileges the transmission of applied knowledge over critical, theoretical and reflexive knowledge.

Research: Knowledge Transfer

While the neoliberal state might have largely resiled from its financial responsibility for public universities, it continues to micromanage them, thereby acting as the driver of the new knowledge economy. It is notable that it has not only orchestrated research to maximize wealth production, but permitted the benefits of that wealth to be privatized. In the process, the state has ceded significant control over knowledge production to the private sector. It is somewhat paradoxical that the resources of public universities are now being used for the private good of corporations, which signifies just how dramatic is the shift away from the values of social liberalism. Technoscience is favoured because it is the most lucrative (Slaughter and Leslie 1997). Claire Polster (1996: 106) observes that the enhanced role of industry in research has had disastrous results for the social sciences and the humanities in Canada because of the way it has skewed research towards industrially related knowledge (see also Axelrod et al. 2001). To this extent, the production of new knowledge is a variation on a theme, following the commodification of teaching.

Knowledge transfer is the key to academic capitalism so far as research is concerned. This means that the outcomes of research cannot be permitted to lie fallow (knowledge for its own sake) within the academy but must be made to serve a useful purpose, such as being deployed to resolve practical problems as a means of generating wealth. The transfer of knowledge to corporations with the capacity to exploit its potential is therefore seen as highly desirable.

In the United States and Britain during the Reagan-Thatcher years, the use of public resources for the benefit of private enterprise rapidly gained in popularity in accordance with the neoliberal agenda (Myoshi 2002: 60). The *Bayh-Dole Act* 1980 in the United States allowed universities themselves to commercialize inventions developed through federally funded research programmes. Universities are therefore intent on forming partnerships with industry to secure research funding in anticipation of future collaboration and commercialization. Encouraging linkages with industry is a key prong of government research policy in Australia (ARC n.d.).

Entrepreneurialism, commercialization and technology transfer have become primary aims of contemporary universities everywhere. The venerable University of Edinburgh is exemplary. Its Strategic Plan (2008–12) specifies three goals: excellence in learning and teaching, excellence in research, and excellence in commercialization and knowledge exchange. What is remarkable is that knowledge transfer and the generation of profits have been elevated to the same status as the traditional university missions of teaching and research. Millions of dollars are being generated from joint enterprises at the University of Edinburgh, as elsewhere.

By constantly emphasizing the economic role of the university, we are moving away from the social justification for its existence, which is the essence of the public good:

> Technology transfer via the patent system is by definition not a public good. The public good aspect remains the conventional one: the outputs of teaching and basic research. (Cowan 2006: 140)

There are also other negative social effects of the economic rationality of neoliberalism, in that making a profit is of preeminent importance and what happens to scholarship and people is incidental. This is the essence of the shift from social to neoliberalism — from the collective good to the right of the few to maximize wealth at the expense of the majority. Ursula Franklin made a similar observation about technical innovation in *Knowledge Reconsidered* (1984: 83). It is in the interstices of the technocratic and profitable that the explanation for the resiling from feminist scholarship can be found.

Academic Capitalism and the Remasculinization of the Academy

I have already noted that new knowledge is more concerned with the transmission of data than the pursuit of wisdom (know-how rather than know-what). Understanding and critiquing new knowledge is not a dimension of the agenda. Hence, the undervaluation of the humanities and the sloughing off of the social have profoundly contracted the traditional spaces for critique (Thornton 2004, 2006). Not only is critique deemed to lack use value in the market, but it is also likely to discomfit corporations that would prefer not to have their business practices exposed. Thus, the pursuit of knowledge for its own sake is out of favour, not only because it is perceived to be unprofitable in terms of knowledge transfer, but because neoliberals are suspicious of its very raison d'être. Law and business are notable examples of the shift away from the prudential towards the applied in their curricular orientation, a factor not without significance at a time of large-scale corporate collapse and corporate greed.

I also believe that the new knowledge economy is deeply gendered, despite its best endeavours to present a neutral façade to the world. Ursula Franklin (1984: 83) similarly noted how the then new technology was grafted onto traditional masculinist notions of power. In one sense, capitalism has little incentive either to eradicate or to encourage racism or sexism (Myoshi 2002: 74), but if the market can deploy sex and sexuality for profits, it will do so (for example, Bulbeck 2006; McRobbie 2007). However, there is an explicit manifestation of antifeminism lurking beneath the surface of the new knowledge economy and embedded in its technologies of power. In this regard, it is not so much the gender of the social actors that drive the present climate as the new ideologies (Lewis 2005: 10).

Kenway et al. capture the subtle incarnation of gender that emerges in their description of the academic subject as *"technopreneurial,"* which refers to the way the favoured techno-scientific knowledge is combined with business acumen (Kenway et al. 2006: 42). They elaborate upon the way the techno-preneur works alone, taking risks and promoting the self, unconcerned about collegiality and the collective good, since the intensification of the economic function of knowledge has come at the expense of the social function.

Picking up on the masculinized character of the technopreneur, Giroux graphically describes the American university post-9/11 as a "militarized knowledge factory" (Giroux 2008; Armitage 2005). He suggests that the hatred of democracy and dissent in an authoritarian neoliberal environment has given rise to a politics of "militarized masculinity," associated particularly with the War in Iraq and the domestic war on terror, which mark the return of the "warrior male":

> whose paranoia is endlessly stoked by the existence of a feminized culture of critical thinking, a gay subculture and a liberal ideology that exhibits a disrespect for top-down order and unquestioned authority and discipline. (Giroux 2008: 61)

Universities as "militarized knowledge factories" are not involved in producing conventional soldiers so much as producing graduate foot soldiers with a uniform habit of mind that happens to be deeply gendered. More is at stake here than simply affirming the stereotypical conjunction between militarism and masculinity. The denigration of the feminine emerged with the populist neoconservative attack on tertiary educated "elites" who were concerned about social justice, rights for Indigenous people, same sex couples and welfare rights (Cahill 2004). It is perhaps unsurprising that this populist form of anti-feminism emerged in the United States, but was replicated in other Anglophone countries, such as Canada and Australia, in new guises (Sawer 2004).

In the attempt to reclaim "authentic manliness" through technocratic new knowledge, critique, once the essence of liberal academic life within these new "knowledge factories," is currently depicted as feminized and dispensable. It is assumed that technocratic and applied knowledge, delivered as information, does not need to be interpreted; it speaks for itself. The most effective way of dispensing with critique is to contract the space that enables it, which is disastrous for projects such as academic feminism, which is necessarily a critical project. The evisceration of this space has enabled anti-feminism to be revived within the new knowledge scripts of the academy even though, as Magda Lewis (2005: 11) points out, terms like patriarchy and sexism have become anachronistic because of the ideological shifts that have occurred. Dorothy Smith observed 25 years ago (1984: 7) that gender does not go away but remains integral to social relations:

> The apparently neutral and impersonal rationality of the ruling apparatus is, in fact, organized by gender. The male subtext concealed beneath its apparently impersonal forms is integral, not accidental.

It is therefore unsurprising that the gendered subtext has adapted to the new circumstances and new ideologies. New knowledge is the apparatus that enables a new form of gender to be produced; new knowledge is not degendered as its technocratic veneer would have us believe. Thus, while the gendered identity of academic subjects no longer appears to count as much as their productivity, the gendered subtext of the new knowledge economy is subtly reified. Competition policy and the logic of the market necessarily produce inequality, not equality, and it is notable that there has been a resiling from the language of equality and equality of opportunity in the academy as well as in public policy more generally (Brodie 2008; Thornton 2008; Summers 2003). The legitimation of inequality tilts the scales permanently in favour of the status quo. In addition, neoliberalism has generally seen an erosion of progressive public interest policies in favour of individualism, which have impacted disproportionately on women (Sawer 2003; Sawer 2006). Promotion of the self through neoliberal rationality has effectively displaced a collective commitment to gender politics in the academy, which has spilled over into the constitution of knowledge.

Conclusion

The transformation of the university through the privatization, corporatization and commercialization of research is not only exerting a profound effect on what is taught, what is researched and what is valued, it is causing the disintegration of the university (Slaughter and Leslie 1997: 243; Wang 2005: 537). Xiaoying Wang suggests that the university will soon "cease to be an institution informed by intellectual autonomy; instead, it will become an appendage of corporations... tailored to the needs of industry and commerce" (2005: 533). In the United States, there is a large number of corporate universities, including McDonalds and Motorola. These giant functionaries are paradigmatic transmitters of new knowledge that are dedicated to serving corporate interests and profit-making, with no interest in critique or the questioning of the knowledge purveyed. What is more, public universities themselves appear to be headed in a similar direction.

How did academics come to accept such a state of affairs with so little resistance? It is not just a question of being directed from above, for they themselves have become "active subjects" in the new regime (Lazzarato 1996: 134). This entails academic subjects managing themselves so that they are ever more productive in ways that best suit the new knowledge economy:

> The fact that immaterial labor produces subjectivity and economic value at the same time demonstrates how capitalist production has invaded our lives and has broken down all the oppositions among economy, power, and knowledge. (Lazzarato 1996: 142)

The web of governmentality in which academic subjects are now enmeshed ensures compliance, for academics inhabit an audit culture that requires constant demonstration of productivity. Resistance may invite disapprobation, disciplinary action and even retrenchment, all of which are salutary disincentives for would-be dissidents. It is conformity, not difference or distinctiveness, which typifies the corporatized university. This has profound implications for academic freedom. It is predicted that the struggle over the meaning and value of knowledge will be a continuing feature of the "education wars" (Olssen and Peters 2005: 340). The corporatization of the university means that this struggle over the nature of knowledge is more likely to take place between management and academics than to be solely an intellectual debate.

The Canadian scholar, Claire Polster (2004: 96), asserts that the only response to university/industry research links is to "get rid of them." However, it is unimaginable that things might revert to the way they were because the higher education sector has come to rely on the wealth generated through academic capitalism.[5] The ploy by neoliberal governments to reduce the operating grants of public universities was a brilliant move, for it guaranteed compliance with the commercialization imperative. Universities had no option but to enter the market. This enabled them to justify fee hikes and questionable liaisons with industry on the ground of necessity, assuaging public criticism with a handful of scholarships and tokenistic gestures in support of the humanities and social sciences. Students — and their parents — also became enmeshed in what one may liken to a system of infeudation. All participants in the system had to defer to those above, while taking responsibility for those below, as well as disciplining the self in terms of the new norms. Hence, I agree with Michael Peters (2002: 165) that, far from being able to end the liaison between public education and business, it is likely to become even stronger:

> In the age of knowledge capitalism, we can expect governments in the West to further ease themselves out of the public provision of education as they begin in earnest to privatize the means of knowledge production and experiment with new businesses and public education at all levels.

All the signs, including the facilitative roles of multinational corporations and supranational bodies, such as the OECD, point in this direction. New knowledge and capital have become so thoroughly entwined within the "knowledge economy", they cannot be disentangled. Within an inordinately short time, feminist knowledge, in all its guises, appears to have become shadowy and elusive within the academy once more.

In light of the way women's voices have been systematically erased within the western intellectual tradition, Dorothy Smith anticipated twenty-five years ago the likelihood of a further period of erasure if an institutional base was not secured for feminist scholarship:

> Without access to this institutional process, we will see again what we have seen in the past: the disappearance of a knowledge of women from the public social discourse. (1984: 11)

For a short time, feminists appeared to have secured an institutional base in the academy as both students and academics, but it turned out to be constructed on quicksand. Since it is primarily as neoliberal subjects that academics are now generally valued, feminist scholars, like their peers, are expected to serve the new knowledge economy rather than critique it. The homologous relationship between feminism and critique means that the contraction of a critical space has necessarily also lead to the contraction of feminism within the academy.

Feminist legal theory, for example, is now rarely offered in law schools in the U.K., New Zealand and Australia. Not only are fewer teachers available to teach the subject, students say they no longer want the word "feminist" to appear on their transcripts as it could jeopardise their job chances.[6] Even if the "F" word is mentioned in a mainstream class, students sigh and put down their pens. As neoliberal subjects, like their teachers in the corporatized academy, these students may have absorbed the applied lesson rather too well.

Feminist studies were abolished at QUT when the Faculty of Arts was closed down because the humanistic and the social were no longer viewed as valuable. Ironically, the replacement Creative Industries Faculty was initially reported as experiencing similar experiences to that of the former faculty. Its teaching program acquired a deficit, there was a high attrition rate and it had difficulty in meeting its marketing promise of preparing graduates to be at the "forefront of entrepreneurial, cultural and creative developments" (Guille 2008). In 2010, it would appear to have overcome its initial teething problems and is offering a varied suite of programs, underpinned by significant industry linkages. However, the appeal to business partners is contingent on the identification of specific marketable skills (QUT n.d.).

Trying to transmute the humanities into an industry in the interest of profit-making does not work. Indeed, it can only do further damage to what is left of the idea of the university. It is imperative that feminist and progressive scholars continue to exercise the vital academic role of critic and conscience of the new knowledge economy, rather than allowing themselves to be reinvented as technopreneurs. Acquiescence in the corporatized role of neoliberal subjects is not only hastening the conversion of universities into giant technological and profit-making institutions in the interests of the state, it is also subtly ensuring their masculinization.

Notes

1. This paper is based on a public lecture presented as the Barbara Betcherman Distinguished Visitor 2008, Osgoode Hall Law School, York University, Toronto, October 15, 2008. I express my gratitude for the generosity of the Betcherman family in funding the visitorship. I would like to thank warmly Professor Mary Jane Mossman for her exceptional hospitality and the Institute for Feminist Legal Studies at Osgoode for hosting my visit. I also acknowledge the research assistance of Dr Trish Luker.
2. Rather than viewing the late twentieth century incarnation of globalization as a new phase of capitalism, Desai (2001) views it as the resumption of the nineteenth century variant with a socialist blip in between.
3. The IMF hosted a major expo in 1998 entitled "The Knowledge Economy." At <imf.org/external/am/1998/expo.htm>
4. Europe and its member states have formulated the goal of making Europe one of the strongest knowledge societies in the world. The Bologna Declaration was a pledge by twenty-nine European countries in 1999 to reform and effect convergence of the structures of higher education. At <ec.europa.eu/education/policies/educ/bologna/bologna.pdf>. See also Commission of the European Communities 2003.
5. Australian universities have become increasingly nervous about the volatility of the lucrative international student market (worth approximately A.U.D. 18 billion

p.a.) because of the instability induced by the global financial crisis, changing immigration and visa policies, and attacks on Indian students (Das and Collins 2010).

6. Interviews conducted with legal academics in 2004–05 for the project "The Neoliberal Legal Academy" (Australian Research Council Discovery Project 0210707).

References

ARC (Australian Research Council). n.d. *Linkage Grants*. At <arc.gov.au/ncgp/lp/lp_default.htm>.

Armitage, John. 2005. "Beyond Hypermodern Militarized Knowledge Factories." *Review of Education, Pedagogy, and Cultural Studies* 27, 3: 219.

Arthurs, H.W. 1998. "The Political Economy of Canadian Legal Education." *Journal of Law & Society* 25, 1: 14.

Axelrod, Paul, Paul Anizef, and Zeng Lin. 2001. "Against All Odds? The Enduring Value of Liberal Education in Universities, Professions, and the Labour Marke.t. *Canadian Journal of Higher Education* 31, 2: 47.

Beck, Ulrich. 1992. *Risk Society: Towards a New Modernity.* (Trans. M. Ritter). London: Sage.

Bousfield, Ann. 1996. "The Voice of Liberal Learning. Is There Still Room for the 'Idea of a University' in 1996?" In Bob Brecher, Otakar Fleischmann and Jo Halliday (eds.), *The University in a Liberal State.* Aldershot Hants: Avebury.

British Academy. 2008. *Punching our Weight: The Humanities and Social Sciences in Public Policy Making.* London: British Academy. At <www.britac.ac.uk>.

Brodie, Janine. 2008. "We Are All Equal now: Contemporary Gender Politics in Canada." *Feminist Theory* 9, 145.

Bulbeck, Chilla. 2006. "Explaining the Generation Debate: Envy, History or Feminism's Victories?" *Lilith* 15, 35.

Burton-Jones, Alan. 1999. *Knowledge Capitalism: Business, Work, and Learning in the New Economy.* Oxford: Oxford University Press.

Cahill, Damien. 2004. "New-Class Discourse and the Construction of Left-Wing Elites." In Marian Sawer and Barry Hindess (eds.), *Us and Them: Anti-Elitism in Australia.* Perth: APII Network, Curtin University of Technology.

Code, Lorraine. 1991. *What Can She Know: Feminist Theory and the Construction of Knowledge.* Ithaca, NY: Cornell University Press.

Commission of the European Communities. 2003. *Communication from the Commission: The Role of the Universities in the Europe of Knowledge* (COM 58 final). Brussels: Commission of the European Communities.

Cowan, Robin. 2006. "Universities and the Knowledge Economy." In Brian Kahim and Dominique Foray (eds.), *Advancing Knowledge and the Knowledge Economy.* Cambridge, MA: MIT Press.

Das, Sushi, and Sarah-Jane Collins. 2010. "Turning Off the Tap." *The Age* (Melbourne), September 15: 11.

Delanty, Gerard. 2002. "The University and Modernity: A History of the Present." In Kevin Robins and Frank Webster (eds.), *The Virtual University? Knowledge, Markets, and Management.* Oxford: Oxford University Press.

Department for Education and Skills, U.K. 2003. *The Future of Higher Education*. London: The Crown.

Desai, Meghnad. 2000. "Globalizing: Neither Ideology Nor Utopia." *Cambridge Review of International Affairs* 14, 1: 16.

___. 2001. "Globalization, Neither Ideology Nor Utopia." At <old.lse.ac.uk/collections/globalDimensions/research/globalizationNeitherIdeologyNorUtopia/Default.htm>.

Epstein, Cynthia Fuchs. 1983. "Women in Sociological Analysis: New Scholarship Versus Old Paradigms." In Elizabeth Langland and Walter Gove (eds.), *A Feminist Perspective in the Academy: The Difference it Makes*. Chicago: University of Chicago Press.

Financial Review (Aust). 2008. "Entire University Campus for Lease: QUT Carseldine Campus, Queensland." September 15: 36.

Fitzgerald, Pat. 1996. "'A Woman Knows These Things': Women's Knowledge and Liberal Education." In Bob Brecher, Otakar Fleischmann and Jo Halliday (eds.), *The University in a Liberal State*. Aldershot Hants: Avebury.

Foray, Dominique. 2006. "Optimizing the Use of Knowledge." In Brian Kahim and Dominique Foray (eds.), *Advancing Knowledge and the Knowledge Economy*. Cambridge, MA: MIT Press.

Franklin, Ursula Martius. 1984. "Will Women Change Technology or Will Technology Change Women?" In Ursula Martius Franklin, Michèle Jean, Sylvia van Kirk, Andrea Levowitz, Meg Luxton, Susan Sherwin and Dorothy E. Smith (eds.), *Knowledge Reconsidered: A Feminist Overview*. Ottawa: Canadian Research Institute for the Advancement of Women.

Franklin, Ursula Martius, Michèle Jean, Sylvia van Kirk, Andrea Levowitz, Meg Luxton, Susan Sherwin and Dorothy E Smith (eds.). 1984. *Knowledge Reconsidered: A Feminist Overview*. Ottawa: Canadian Research Institute for the Advancement of Women.

Freire, Paolo. 1996. *Pedagogy of the Oppressed*. (Trans. M.B. Ramos). New York: Continuum.

Giroux, Henry A. 2008. "The Militarization of U.S. Higher Education After 9/11." *Theory Culture Society* 25: 56.

Guille, Howard. 2008. "The Last Post — Humanities at QUT: Introduction." *Journal of the Public University* 5. At <publicuni.org/journal/home.html>.

Hayek, Friedrich. 1937. "Economics and Knowledge." *Econimica IV*, 33.

___. 1945. "The Use of Knowledge in Society." *American Economic Review* 35, 4: 519. At <hayekcenter.org/friedrichhayek/hayek.html>.

Johnstone, D. Bruce, with Alka Arora and William Experton. 1998. *The Financing and Management of Higher Education: A Status Report on Worldwide Reforms*. New York: World Bank.

Kahim, Brian, and Dominique Foray (eds.). 2006. *Advancing Knowledge and the Knowledge Economy*. Cambridge, MA: MIT Press.

Kenway, Jane, Elizabeth Bullen, Johannah Fahey, with Simon Robb. 2006. *Haunting the Knowledge Economy*. London: Routledge.

Keohane, Nannerl O. 1983. "Speaking from Silence: Women and the Science of Politics." In Elizabeth Langland and Walter Gove (eds.), *A Feminist Perspective in the Academy: The Difference It Makes*. Chicago: University of Chicago Press.

Krause, Kerri-Lee, Robyn Hartley, Richard James and Craig McInnes. 2005. *The First Year Experience in Australian Universities: Findings from a Decade of National Studies*. Canberra: Australian Government.

Langland, Elizabeth, and Walter Gove. 1983. "Editors' Notes." In Elizabeth Langland and Walter Gove (eds.), *A Feminist Perspective in the Academy: The Difference it Makes*. Chicago: University of Chicago Press.

___. 1983. *A Feminist Perspective in the Academy: The Difference it Makes*. Chicago: University of Chicago Press.

Lazzarato, Maurizio. 1996. "Immaterial Labor." In Paolo Virno and Michael Hardt (eds.), *Radical Thought in Italy: A Potential Politics*. Minneapolis: University of Minnesota Press.

Lewis, Magda. 2005. "More than Meets the Eye: The Under Side of the Corporate Culture of Higher Education and Possibilities for a New Feminist Critique." *Journal of Curriculum Theorizing* 2, 1: 7.

Lovink, Geert, and Ned Rossiter (eds.). 2007. *My Creativity Reader: A Critique of Creative Industries*. Amsterdam: Institute of Network Cultures.

LSE Public Policy Group. 2008. "Maximizing the Social, Policy and Economic Impacts of Research in the Humanities and Social Sciences: Research Report." (Supplementary Report.) London: London School of Economics and Political Sciences. At <britac.ac.uk/reports/impact/index/cfm>.

Lyotard, Jean Francois. 1984. *The Postmodern Condition: A Report on Knowledge*. Manchester: Manchester University Press.

Marginson, Simon, and Mark Considine. 2000. *The Enterprise University: Power, Governance and Reinvention in Australia*. Cambridge: Cambridge University Press.

McRobbie, Angela. 2007. "Top Girls?" *Cultural Studies* 21, 4: 718.

Miyoshi, Masao. 2002. "The University in the "Global" Economy." In Kevin Robins and Frank Webster (eds.), *The Virtual University? Knowledge, Markets, and Management*. Oxford: Oxford University Press.

Newman, Frank, Lara Couturier, and Jamie Scurry. 2004. *The Future of Higher Education: Rhetoric, Reality, and the Risks of the Market*. San Francisco: Jossey-Bass.

Newman, John Henry. [1852] 1976. *The Idea of a University*. (Ed. and intro. I.T. Ker). Oxford: Clarendon.

Nicholson, Carol. 1995. "Postmodern Feminisms." In Michael Peters (ed.), *Education and the Postmodern Condition*. Westport, CT: Bergin & Garvey.

Noble, David F. 2001. *Digital Diploma Mills: The Automation of Higher Education*. New York: Monthly Review Press.

Nowotny, Helga, Peter Scott, and Michael Gibbons. 2001. *Re-Thinking Science: Knowledge and the Public in an Age of Uncertainty*. Cambridge: Polity.

Olssen, Mark, and Michael A. Peters. 2005. "Neoliberalism, Higher Education and the Knowledge Economy: From the Free Market to Knowledge Capitalism." *Journal of Education Policy* 20, 3: 313.

Peters, Michael. 2002. "Universities, Globalization and the Knowledge Economy." *Southern Review* 35, 2: 16.

Polster, Claire. 1996. "Dismantling the Liberal University: The State's New Approach to Academic Research." In Bob Brecher, Otakar Fleischmann and Jo Halliday (eds.), *The University in a Liberal State*. Aldershot Hants: Avebury.

___. 2004. "Rethinking and Remaking Academic Freedom." In Denise Doherty-

Delorme and Erika Shaker (eds.), *Missing Pieces V: An Alternative Guide to Canadian Post-Secondary Education*. Ottawa: Canadian Centre for Policy Alternatives.

QUT (Queensland University of Technology), Creative Industries Faculty. n.d. *Industry and Community Connections.* At <creativeindustries.qut.edu.au/industry-community/connections>.

Readings, Bill. 1996. *The University in Ruins*. Cambridge, MA: Harvard University Press.

Rowland, Stephen. 2006. *The Enquiring University: Compliance and Contestation in Higher Education*. Maidenhead Berks: Society for Research into Higher Education & Open University Press.

___. 2008. "Collegiality and Intellectual Love." *British Journal of Sociology of Education* 29, 3: 353.

Ryan, Alan. 1998. *Liberal Anxieties and Liberal Education*. New York: Hill & Wang.

Sawer, Marian. 2004. "Populism and Public Choice in Australia and Canada: Turning Equality-Seekers into 'Special Interests'." In Marian Sawer and Barry Hindess (eds.), *Us and Them: Anti-Elitism in Australia*. Perth: APII Network, Curtin University of Technology.

___. 2006. "From Women's Interests to Special Interests: Reframing Equality Claims." In L. Chappel and L. Hill (eds.), *The Politics of Women's Interests*. London: Routledge.

Slaughter, Sheila, and Larry L Leslie. 1997. *Academic Capitalism: Politics, Policies, and the Entrepreneurial University* Baltimore: Johns Hopkins.

Smith, Dorothy E. 1984. "The Renaissance of Women." In Ursula Franklin, Michèle Jean, Sylvia van Kirk, Andrea Levowitz, Meg Luxton, Susan Sherwin and Dorothy E. Smith (eds.), *Knowledge Reconsidered: A Feminist Overview.* Ottawa: Canadian Research Institute for the Advancement of Women.

___. 1988. *The Everyday World as Problematic: A Feminist Sociology.* Milton Keynes: Open University Press.

___. 1990. *Texts, Facts, and Femininity: Exploring the Relations of Ruling.* London: Routledge.

Summers, Anne. 2003. *The End of Equality: Work, Babies and Women's Choices in the 21st Century*. Sydney: Random House.

Thornton. Margaret. 2004. "Neoliberal Melancholia: The Case of Feminist Legal Scholarship." *Australian Feminist Law Journal* 20, 7.

___. 2006. "The Dissolution of the Social in the Legal Academy." *Australian Feminist Law Journal* 25, 3.

___. 2007. "The Law School, the Market and the New Knowledge Economy." *Legal Education Review* 17, 1 & 2: 1.

___. 2008. "The Evisceration of EEO in Higher Education." *Australian Universities Review* 50, 2: 59.

University of Edinburgh. 2009–12. *Strategic Plan 2008–2012*. At <docs.sasg.ed.ac.uk/gasp/strategicplanning/StrategicPlan.pdf>.

Veblen, Thorstein. [1918] 1954. *The Higher Learning in America: A Memorandum on the Conduct of Universities by Business Men*. Stanford: Academic Reprints.

Wang, Xiaoying. 2005. "Farewell to the Humanities." *Rethinking Marxism* 17, 4: 525.

World Bank. 1994. *World Bank Report: The Lessons of Experience*. Washington, DC:

World Bank.

____. 2007. *Building Knowledge Economies: Advanced Strategies for Development.* Washington, DC: World Bank.

Yarrow, Megan. 2010. "Review of *MyCreativity Reader: A Critique of Creative Industries.*" At <reviews.media-culture.org.au>.

Chapter Five

THE UNIVERSITY-ON-THE-GROUND
Reflections on the Canadian Experience

Janice Newson

A few years ago I interviewed feminist sociologist Dorothy Smith for a collection of essays on visions of the university. I asked how her vision of the university has fared through the many changes that have taken place in the Canadian university over the course of her career — from the late 1950s and 1960s expansion of higher education, to the funding cutbacks of the 70s and early 80s, to the shift in the late 80s and onward toward the university pursuing an increasingly corporate and commercial direction.

"Some changes I see as very positive," Smith responded, "changes that have come about from struggles we have made in the women's movement and struggles people have made against racism. I don't want to idealize the results of these struggles but if I think back thirty years, the effects have been huge. They are major gains" (Smith 2010: 74).

I thought of Smith's response recently when my department in the new Faculty of Liberal Arts and Professional Studies at York University was revising its constitution to accommodate the merger of two sociology departments. A clause in the old constitution required that the women faculty, if they choose, be entitled to name a woman representative to all departmental standing committees until such time as the proportion of tenure stream faculty women reaches 50 percent. As a member of the constitution sub-committee, it was my job to move that this clause be deleted because the 50 percent target had been exceeded for some time. But when I did so, I felt compelled to remind the many younger faculty members and graduate students present that this was an historic moment in that the adoption of this clause back in the 1980s had resulted from a long struggle by a small handful of primarily faculty women. Were it not for winning this struggle, as well as others aimed at establishing minimum quota for hiring women throughout the university, the overall gender balance that York celebrates today would not exist.

Smith's comments and the change in my department's constitution are testimonials to an important transformation of the university in Canada that took place over the past forty years, from it being relatively enclosed, elitist, and patriarchal to it being more open, accessible, and inclusive, particularly in terms of the gender balance and to a lesser degree, the ethnic diversity of its student body and faculty complement. Often in celebratory prose, some commentators have referred to this development as the feminization of the academy. Women have not only acquired majority status in many social science and humanities disciplines and previously male dominated professional schools such as medicine and law, but they have also entered the ranks of senior administration, including the office of university president.

To be sure, reports still abound of chilly climates toward women. Women remain under-represented in the senior professorial ranks, in many physical sciences and technology-based disciplines and on lists of winners of high-ranking academic awards, and members of minority groups have some distance to go in emulating the gains that women academics have achieved. But to recast Smith's assessment, feminist struggle has helped to significantly change the landscape of the Canadian university in ways that can not be easily reversed: whole new disciplines have been established, new lines of highly valued scholarship have been launched, and, by extending the concepts of inclusion and equity to their own struggles, other under-represented and minority groups have gained access to university education and academic careers. By any standard, feminists have good reason to celebrate the fact that their transformative impulse has, over a relatively few decades, worked its way through, and helped to reshape, an influential educational and cultural institution.

However, this story of progressive social and institutional change is not the only tale to tell of the university's development over the past fifty years. Especially from the mid-1970s onward, universities have been on a trajectory of increasingly justifying their existence in terms of wealth creation and contributing toward private sector innovation and economic productivity in the global marketplace. Scholars and commentators on higher education, some as critics, some as advocates and others claiming a purely analytical perspective on this shift in the university's direction, have adopted terms such as corporatization, marketization, commercialization, as well as others to capture this path of development (Chan and Fisher 2008; Fisher and Rubenson 1998; Newson 1998; Newson and Buchbinder 1988, 1990; Newson and Polster 2010; Polster 1996, 1998; Turk 2000; Woodhouse 2009).

As we look at the Canadian university-on-the-ground in the light of these parallel trajectories of development, troubling questions need to be asked and qualifications appended to the advancements described above. Feminists and other groups who have gained access to the university as a vehicle for pursuing progressive agendas might well ask, to what kind of institution have we gained access. How, if at all, have their progressive agendas been affected by corporatization? Even more provocatively, have their bids for access to, and influence in, academic communities been implicated in the shift of the university toward more commercially oriented endeavours?

In the early 1990s, I attended a status of women event sponsored by the Canadian Association of University Teachers. I grew a bit queasy when I overheard a colleague say over coffee to another, "How much of the usual women's paraphernalia have you acquired on your campus — you know, sexual harassment centre, affirmative action programme, equal employment officer, status of women's office?" My attention was caught not just by the use of "paraphernalia" to refer to important institutional changes, nor by the ho-hum "haven't things become routine" tone. It was that I had been noticing in recent months that postings of this so-called paraphernalia had begun to appear on university websites and in glossy in-house public relations magazines, as though to present the image of a women friendly environment. In spite of the fact that the under-pinning of this image had been struggled for over decades by committed women faculty often through their faculty associations and unions, university administrations now appeared to be claiming bragging rights to women friendliness as a sign of their progressive managerial practices. In light of the increasing pressures on universities to solve their funding shortfalls through selling their services to corporate and other types of paying clientele, might these postings be intended to serve as the good housekeeping seal of approval to attract these potential clients?

I felt pressed after this encounter to think on how the noteworthy gains of academic women's struggles interacted with changes in institutional practice associated with the corporate agenda for universities. What does it mean for academic women's concerns generally when, for example, in pursuit of a woman positive, good-for-business image, senior administrations and Boards of Governors promote female diversity in the management team? What does it mean for feminist work to be afforded institutional recognition and support when it is organized into a research grant and client-seeking research institute, while at the same time, loss of control over class sizes and increasing work loads make it difficult to implement a feminist pedagogy in classrooms or to offer a reliable programme of women's studies courses? What does it mean for many areas of the university's student body and teaching faculty to be feminized when undergraduates in these same areas are being taught by an increasingly casualized, primarily female, faculty work force?

The chapter that follows will not specifically answer these questions but it will provide a context in which to address them in the future. It was originally given as a lecture in 2005 to an international seminar in Puerto Rico, where invited scholars of higher education from five countries were asked to map out the policy developments that had shaped their university sectors over the past several decades.[1] The chapter provides an overview of how the university in Canada has responded to developments in funding policies that have promoted the corporatization trajectory. It allows readers to think about how, and to what degree, the progressive changes in universities that are rightfully to be celebrated have been, and continue to be, contextualized by other changes that have taken place over the same time period. Hopefully such reflection will offer insight to those who will be involved in shaping the next few decades of university development, alerting them to what has given shape to the institutions in which they continue struggles for progressive social change.

General Perspective

My work on the university places less emphasis on analyzing policies per se and more on how policies are taken up and enacted by individuals and groups within academic institutions. I believe that the responses of academic communities and their members to government policies have been necessary vehicles for accomplishing what others and I conceive to be a fundamental transformation in universities. Correspondingly, my work has attempted more to influence members of the academic community about their role in enacting specific policies than to influence policy makers directly.

One way to influence academics is to make visible how these policies are shaping their own teaching and research practices as well as the practices of the institutions in which they carry them out. While I do not dismiss the sociological importance of policy discourse, I am more interested in how the university-on-the-ground has responded to policy changes than in the policies themselves.

I follow this tack in this chapter. I will briefly overview the key turns and summarize the ways the Canadian university on the whole and on-the-ground has responded to them. Then I will focus more closely on three recent policy initiatives that build upon, and continue the trajectory of, the policy interventions that preceded them. I focus on these three initiatives because they constitute an aggressive intervention by the federal government that strongly induces universities to transform themselves into knowledge businesses[2] that are networked into a global higher-education industry. I will conclude with a discussion of concerns that arise out of the university's responses to these policy initiatives.

Retrenching, Retrofitting and Re-Positioning Canadian Universities, 1975-1995

It is only recently that policy makers have begun to understand the critical links between expenditure patterns, cost and efficiency in higher education and the mechanisms by which institutions receive funds… Many governments now see financial incentives as a more effective way *of influencing the pattern of activities in higher education institutions* than administrative intervention. (Zinberg 1991: 45, emphasis mine)

Fiscal Retrenchment

By the late 1970s, fiscal restraint had become the priority of Canadian public sector funding policy. Earlier in the decade, both provincial and federal governments had begun to reduce the rate of growth of funds allocated to the higher education sector. Combined with inflationary pressures and increased enrolments, universities across the country began to experience financial shortfalls to varying degrees. On the whole, the university community tended to respond to these financial pressures as temporary — a condition that had to be endured for now. Eventually, it was believed, things would return to normal, meaning to the expansion that had characterized the post-war period.

Even so, for institutions that for well over a decade had been in the groove of building new programs, hiring new faculty and enrolling more and more students, the relatively shallow budget cuts that were required in the early stages of restraint were crisis inducing. Most universities during this period experienced internal conflicts within the academic-administrative leadership — deans versus deans, deans versus presidents — as well as between the academic-administrative leadership and the faculty. Beginning around the middle of the 1970s in Anglo-Canada and earlier in Québec, the faculty had begun to adopt collective bargaining strategies, sometimes as unions under labour legislation and sometimes through special plans collective bargaining. Their aim was to secure their terms and conditions of employment against the threat of declining budgets and also to preserve collegial governance in the face of increasingly assertive and expanding administrations.

By the early 1980s, the temporary funding shortfalls had unfolded into chronic under funding and the task of managing the budget began to assume a central place in planning and decision making. Along with it, the role of the administration began to transform incrementally but decidedly into management. Compared to the style of academic administration that had become institutionalized during the post-war expansion of higher education, a notion of management advocated by George Keller began to take hold. It includes a strategically-oriented style of leadership that takes charge of the university by setting the path for its development, devising strategic plans and measurable objectives and creating the necessary financial and organizational mechanisms for realizing them (Keller 1983). In other words, management initiates policy as opposed to implementing decisions made in collegial bodies such as senates and faculty councils.

By the end of the decade, an array of practices that are now identified in critical literature as either intrinsic to, or associated with, managerialism had begun to infuse most if not all Canadian universities (Newson 1992; Hardy 1996). These practices include:

- Embedding efficiency, accountability and productivity as primary criteria for all decision making;
- Fragmenting the academic workforce by creating separate classes of academic appointments with distinct terms and conditions of employment (for example, full-time tenure stream, full-time contractually limited, single course contracts) as a means of achieving cost efficiencies;
- Appropriating to newly expanded administrative offices, policy-making activities that had been carried out by faculty members as part of their service function;
- Instituting forms of documentary-based decision making whose parameters are designed and controlled by managerial priorities and relevancies, such as mission statements and five-year plans;
- Orienting institutional decisions toward the expectations of external constituencies such as government, business, funding agencies and community organizations; and
- Measuring academic activities in terms of input and output to assess the relative cost efficiency of, and demand for, these activities.

Accompanying this growth of managerialism was a corresponding decline in the influence of collegial bodies in university decision making. Academic criteria and academic assessment became less significant in planning exercises, designing programs and managing the day-to-day operations of academic units. By the late 1980s, academics collectively (through bodies like senates, faculty council, departments and faculty associations and unions) had become relatively marginal participants in the decisions that had major consequences for the academic direction of their institutions.

The fiscal restraint created by changes in government funding policies was not the only impetus to the growth of managerialism and the corresponding decline in faculty influence, however. Beginning in the early 1980s, a second phase of policy intervention overlapped with fiscal retrenchment — university-corporate linking.

University-Corporate Linking
It is ironic that policies promoting greater collaboration between universities and corporations were first presented as a kind of rescue effort, promising to relieve university communities from declining morale and annual crises associated with budgetary short-falls. In 1984, the inaugural report of the Corporate Higher Forum,[3] an organization founded in 1983 by two McGill university professors, articulated the benefits of university-corporate collaboration to universities and corporations (Maxwell and Currie 1984). Universities would

acquire new sources of funding to counteract government under-funding, and corporations would gain much needed expertise — a window on science — to enhance their competitive edge in the international marketplace.

Throughout the 1980s and early 1990s, the research funding policies developed by the federal government supported the policy direction advocated by the Corporate-Higher Education Forum almost as though it was following a beacon (Buchbinder and Newson 1990; Polster 1994). These policies included:

- Allocating federal monies through the three national research councils to targeted research programs and to matched grant research programs that required research partnerships between academic researchers and (primarily) private sector corporate funders;
- Allocating federal monies to establish new institutions on campus that were designed to attract and facilitate university-corporate research partnerships, such as Industrial Liaison Offices and Technology Transfer Centres;
- Establishing Centres of Excellence Networks that brought together academic and industrial researchers to work on research areas designated by governments as high priority. Some provincial governments funded their own centres of excellence programs as well; and
- Changing legislation to allow private ownership of the intellectual property rights to knowledge created through federally funded research grants.

Critics faced a number of difficulties challenging this new policy direction.[4] For one thing, no public debate took place about the merits of the policy direction even though it represented a significant change in ideas about the university as a public institution in Canadian society. Instead, specific policies were adopted incrementally and pragmatically without opening them to critical assessment either in the academic community or the public more generally. Moreover, public bodies such as the three national research councils on which academics were strongly represented at the time, helped to implement rather than resist these policies. They justified their actions on the grounds that not co-operating with government might lead to deeper cuts to their basic research budgets (Newson 1996). To the extent that debate took place at all, it occurred in small committees out of the hearing of either the public at large or the academic community generally and, given the specific mandates of such committees, it focused mainly on details rather than on the policy direction as a whole.

For another thing, most academics were unaware that these developments were taking place. Visible manifestations of the policies — campus buildings renamed for corporate donors, in-house research businesses, commercial advertisements — did not emerge until the mid-1990s, by which time both the organizational, procedural and legislative changes necessary to support this policy direction were already entrenched.

But perhaps the most important reason that the academic community as a whole did not challenge these policies is that most members of the academic community believed that these new opportunities for improved research funding were the only game in town. After a decade and a half of fiscal restraint, both university administrations and individual academics chose to take from them what they could to support their ongoing activities.

Consequently, by the end of the 1980s, significant changes in the university-on-the-ground had begun to take place. New structures emerged which began to assume a central place in achieving the shifting objectives of the university, as though they were parts of a shadow institution growing parasitically off the traditional one including, for example, spin-off companies, centres of excellence, innovation centres, centres of technology transfer and other units that embodied the idea of corporate-university collaboration. They began to draw upon the university's resources while aspects of the traditional university began to shrink or disappear.

Policies of fiscal restraint and corporate linking thus interacted as pump primers. Continued under-funding was a powerful lever for seducing or pushing universities in the direction of corporate partnerships. At the same time, universities' responses to these enticements and pressures reinforced the expansion of managerial controls. Industrially relevant science required infrastructural arrangements and cultures that differed from the collegial arrangements and cultures of academic communities — such as the need for secrecy, quick decision-making, and responsiveness to changing market pressures. An assertive and strategically oriented administration acting independently of collegial bodies could expeditiously negotiate contracts with corporate partners and develop them in a spirit compatible with the needs of private sector business.

Taken together, changes in Canadian universities that were commensurate with university-corporate linking and fiscal restraint were not merely add-ons to the university-as-it-is: they were transformative. Managerialism served as a methodology through which universities could maximize their efficiency, cost-effectiveness and present themselves as accountable businesses. Linking academic resources to corporate objectives through specific contracts and partnership arrangements both required and legitimized a practical conception of knowledge as intellectual property, a commodity that could be privately owned and protected from unpaid for use through patenting and licensing agreements. Through these changes, the focus of the university's role in creating and disseminating knowledge began to shift from serving broadly defined social purposes and public constituencies — in other words, the common good or the public interest — to serving market-oriented purposes for targeted and private clienteles or customers.

However, these overlapping policies of fiscal restraint and university-corporate linking did not cohere well in the university-on-the-ground: they posed opportunities and constraints that conflicted with each other, feeding some parts of the university while starving others, and often fueling internal tensions and political struggles. For example, while the federal government was allocating funds to targeted and partnered research, provincial governments' were under-funding teaching programs and the routine operational costs of maintaining university facilities. Moreover, funding flowed disproportionately into research areas in the natural, physical and new technology-based sciences — areas deemed by government to be of high priority to the new economy. Areas in the social sciences and humanities, seen to be less relevant to corporate growth and innovation, were more likely to feel the full pressures of provincial governments' fiscal restraint policies. Universities were therefore trapped between contradictory and competing pressures from these two levels of policy intervention. They had to coordinate and re-balance their responses to constantly changing policies coming from each level of government. I will return to this point in the final section of this chapter.

Perhaps the most significant transformation in Canadian universities was a change in their political and intellectual positioning as public institutions. In contrast to collegially governed institutions which received their programmatic direction largely from the political and intellectual currents that operated within them, the corporate-linked, cost efficient and economically accountable universities that began to emerge in the early to mid 1990s were more attuned to the outside and were thus responsive not only to corporate demands, but also to the programmatic interventions of granting agencies and government ministries. In other words, corporate-linked universities were plugged into external economic and political agents and agendas that increasingly shaped if not determined their educational and research objectives. By the early to mid 1990s, it was possible to argue that Canadian universities to varying degrees had begun to exist in the world less as distinctively academic and educational institutions and more as business organizations that sell knowledge-based products to paying customers and targeted markets.

Launching Canadian Universities as Knowledge Businesses in the Global Knowledge Industry: 1995 to the Present

> Just as the research university emerged in Canada at the start of the twentieth century, perhaps a new species, the service university, is evolving in the last decades. In such an institution teaching and research would not be displaced so much as they would be re-oriented. *The essence of such a university would be a dynamic, integral relationship with society.* Just as the research university underwent structural and functional change, so too will the service university. (Enros and Farley 1986: 16, emphasis mine)

Prior to the 1990s, policy makers, university administrators and faculty members, to the extent that they were aware, tended to either deny or down-play the idea that universities were being transformed by a corporate agenda. But by the mid-1990s, not only were there visible signs on university campuses of a growing corporate presence but also, public policy statements and university publications of all kinds unapologetically and without qualification adopted the language and conception of universities as businesses. Nor did they back away from associating publicly funded universities with profit-making activities.

Interestingly, this flagrant and often flamboyant celebration of the university's recent conversion to the practices and objectives of business has been matched by a literature increasingly critical of it as a global trend in higher education policy, even though writers in different national contexts have utilized different terminologies and theoretical approaches to support their critiques. Sheila Slaughter and Larry Leslie have conceived of the changes taking place in U.S. universities and other national jurisdictions in terms of academic capitalism. Australian scholars, most notably Simon Marginson, have employed a conceptualization of marketization rooted in Foucauldian scholarship. Henry Etzkowitz has advanced the triple helix of universities, governments and corporations based on the economic theories of Joseph Schumpeter. Canadian scholarship including my own has employed the terms corporatization and commercialization to analyze these trends, signaling the growing corporate influence on, and commercial orientation of, research and teaching activities on Canadian campuses.

Corporatization, however, is commonly used in a narrow, unidirectional sense, implying if not out-rightly claiming that the corporate elite in general has seized control of the university's resources through their financial donations and their dominant role on boards of governors. They argue that particular pharmaceutical, agri-business, resource extraction, biotechnology, and computer technology firms have gained an unseemly foothold in specific university faculties and research units (Tudiver 1999).

I agree that these influences exist and that they have grown substantially since university-corporate collaboration became a policy emphasis in the mid 1980s. However, the complexity of what is happening is not sufficiently captured by one-sided unmediated influences flowing from external business interests into the university. Rather than as one-way processes of influence, corporatization and commercialization are better understood as two-way, multidimensional processes mediated by the political interests of governments and the professional and administrative interests of individual as well as collective agents within the academic community. One set of processes involves the movement into universities of economic and political influences that, in previous times, were considered external to their programmatic development; and the other involves the movement outward by universities to commercialize their services and market them to specific clienteles and customers. These inward and outward movements encapsulate the dual nature of the university's changing relationship to social, economic and political agents in both the private and public sectors of Canadian society.

In this, the university has been an agent in its own right. Rather than mechanically adapting to pressures, it has actively engaged in the ordering of these relationships, giving them concrete form through changing their own practices and orientations. The corporatization of universities and the commercialization of their research and teaching activities are thus enabled not just by government policies that support a particular model of economic innovation favouring corporate-sector interests. They are also enabled by a re-orientation within universities toward creating and disseminating knowledge as a commodity for targeted markets and clienteles, and adopting business practices as their *modus operandi*: in other words, transforming themselves into knowledge businesses.

A new array of government policies adopted since the mid-1990s are building on these developments. These policies treat universities more forthrightly as knowledge businesses that need to be regulated and integrated into a larger Canadian knowledge industry. Of particular significance are three initiatives undertaken by the federal government: the Canadian Foundation for Innovation (CFI), The Millennial Chairs Programme (or the Canadian Research Chairs Programme, CRC), and the Framework Agreement of 2002 which implements several key recommendations of the 1999 Report of the Expert Panel on the Commercialization of Academic Research.

The Canadian Foundation for Innovation (CFI) and The Millennial Chairs Programme (CRC)

In 1997, the federal government's new budget allocated almost one billion dollars to update the Canadian research infrastructure. This budget was subsequently expanded to 3.15 billion dollars through to 2010. Rather than following the long established practice of distributing these funds to academic researchers through the three existing research councils — the Natural Sciences and Engineering Research Council (NSERC), the Social Sciences and Humanities Research Council (SSHRC) and the Canadian Institutes for Health Research (CIHR, formally the Medical Research Council) — an independent crown corporation called the Canada Foundation for Innovation was created to allocate these funds not to individual researcher applicants but to institutional applicants. It consists of a Board of Directors, including government appointed academics and a substantial number of corporate executives who are responsible for setting policies and designing programs to achieve the foundation's objective of promoting state of the art research in Canadian universities as well as other research institutions. In order to receive funds under this program, the applying institutions must have partners that will provide 60 percent of the total cost of the proposed infrastructural developments.

In 1999, the same federal government allocated just under one billion dollars over five years to fund 2,000 Canada research chairs to generate research excellence by supporting the work of emerging and established star researchers. While these chairs are theoretically for all areas of research, the programme in fact allocates the funds on a proportional basis: 45 percent to the natural sciences and engineering, 35 percent to health and 20 percent to the social sciences and humanities.

The CFI and CRC programs mark a significant turning point in research funding for at least two reasons. First, they have inserted a massive dose of federal monies — over four billion dollars — into a university system that has suffered from government under funding for well over two decades. Moreover, they insert these substantial funds disproportionately into areas identified as relevant to economic growth and innovation. Taken together they have the potential to reshape significantly the balance of disciplines and programs in local institutions and to focus more narrowly the educational and research objectives of the university system across the country in ways that are compatible with the economic objectives of the federal government.

Claire Polster (2002) argues that the introduction of the CFI and CRC programs are a significant break in the federal government's past approach to research funding in several important ways, three of which I emphasize here:

- Local institutions' shares of CFI funds and CRC positions are determined by an institution's, rather than individual researchers', previous track records, based on their success in securing research funds from the three national research councils;
- Applicants to the CFI and CRC programs are universities, rather than individual academics or groups of academics; and

- Assessments of applications for these programs take into account local institutions' strategic planning documents rather than the intellectual and research priorities of individual academics or groups of academics, thus tying the initiatives of individual academics and associated academic units to the strategic management agendas of their institutions.

Universities are highly motivated to compete for these awards because (a) the amount of funds allocated through these programs is substantial; (b) as Polster points out, the size of the awards are higher than those received through other programs; and (c) the relative positioning of local institutions within Canada is highlighted by the number of awards they receive from these programs. Polster argues that, through their participation in the CFI and CRC programs, Canadian universities will become more in tune with, and equipped for, advancing Canada's position in the global knowledge-based economy because the federal government's economic innovation agenda is built into their criteria and because government officials and appointees have influence over decisions made within these programs (Polster 1996: 276–79).

Polster predicts that by involving themselves these programs, each university will step up their competition with all other Canadian universities not only to acquire CFI and CRC awards but also to improve their relative ranking, since their entitlement to a greater or lesser share of the resources is determined by their overall success in research funding competitions. In setting their own courses of action, universities will thus become much more attentive to, and take more into account, the inner workings of other universities and their strategies for improving their rank. She also predicts that local universities' autonomy vis-à-vis government will be more limited. For one thing, the CFI and CRC programs require universities to organize their priorities around strategically selected focus areas as determined by their institutional strategic plan, rather than around, for example, the intellectual and research priorities of their front line researchers and academic units. For another thing, the highest decision making bodies of the CFI and CRC programs composed as it is of government officials and appointees "exercise *de facto* veto over university proposals" (Polster 2002: 283) and there is no provision to appeal these decisions.

Polster shows how the CFI and CRC programs may also lead to significant transformations in the relations between the government and the private sector, and between universities and the private sector. She concludes,

> it is not clear that CFI and CRC programs, as presently constituted, will produce academic research that is radically different from that which currently exists. It is clear, however, that they will stimulate

some radical changes in relations among and between all of the parties involved in academic research… [and] given the significance of these shifts these programs may end up having more impacts, and more profound impacts, on academic research than their creators ever imagined or intended. (Polster 2002: 296)

The Expert Panel on the Commercialization of Academic Research and the 2002 Framework Agreement

Two other recent public policy initiatives undertaken by the federal government provide further insight to how the relatively massive influx of research funding made available through the CFI and CRC programs may have significant implications for local universities as emerging knowledge businesses.

In 1996, the federal government created the Prime Minister's Advisory Council on Science and Technology to review Canada's performance in research and innovation, to identify issues of national concern and to advise on a forward-looking agenda that would position Canada in the international context (at <ACST-CCST.gc.ca/home_e.html>, modified September 13, 2004). To proceed with its mandate, the Council created several expert panels one of which was The Expert Panel on the Commercialization of Research. The panel consisted of nine expert members including technology transfer practitioners from Canada and the U.S., venture capitalists and other representatives from government and industry. As described in a report published in *University Affairs*, a monthly publication of the Association of Universities and Colleges of Canada (AUCC), the panel is heavily weighted toward industry (Berkowitz 1999).

An August 1999 news release by the Natural Sciences and Engineering Research Council (NSERC) describes the objective of the Expert Panel's recommendations as follows:

> The objective of the recommendations is to provide the greatest possible economic return to Canadian taxpayers on the investments they make in university research. This research takes the form of new economic activity when research results produce new high value-added goods and services. Commercialization of university research creates good jobs and social benefits, for example, through improvements in health care made possible by the application of medical research discoveries. (NSERC 1999)

Among other things, the report recommends:

- That the federal government invest fifty million dollars, which represents 5 percent of what it already invests in university research, to enable universities to commercialize intellectual property;

- That, in exchange for these increased funds, universities annually report to government on any federally funded intellectual property (IP) that has commercial potential;
- That universities adopt a flexible policy toward ownership of IP, but where federally funded researchers want to commercialize the IP they own, that the IP be disclosed and assigned to universities;
- That universities be allowed to assign IP to affiliated research institutions, private sector corporations and other researchers under specified conditions, including when another partner will be better able to maximize returns to Canada without undue conflicts of interest; and
- That changes be made in taxation on personal income, capital gains and employee stock options so that "start-up companies and established businesses that are dependent on universities as a source of innovation can grow" (Polster 2002: 297).

The most controversial recommendation of the Expert Panel is that commercialization be named the fourth mission of the university, along with teaching, research and service to the community. The panel defended this recommendation by arguing that there is a strong cultural bias against innovation in some university departments and "potential innovators are afraid of putting their academic careers in jeopardy" (NSERC 1999).

The federal government has not enacted these recommendations as a whole package — but that is not unusual and it does not mean that the individual recommendations or the thrust of the package are moot. Recommendations of reports are often incorporated into a variety of specific policies and practices, often in modified form and on a piece-meal basis. In fact, since the Expert Panel submitted its report in May of 1999, its influence has been reflected in both federal and provincial public policy initiatives.

For example, in the 2001 budget, the federal government affirmed its intention to promote increased commercialization of the research that it funds. The 2002 Speech from the Throne committed the government to pursue a permanent solution to indirect costs of research for universities and strategies for research commercialization. In 2003, the governments of Canada and Ontario each contributed 20 million dollars to a new Medical and Related Sciences Centre (MaRS) whose total cost was projected to be 345 million dollars. More telling was the ceremonial rhetoric that accompanied the federal government's announcement of these funds. An Industry Canada press release described the centre as a research and development facility "*designed to accelerate the commercialization of innovative academic research* in areas such as biotechnology, medical devices and genetics" (Industry Canada 2003, emphasis mine). Alan J. Rock, then Minister of Industry, stated that "The resources at MaRS *will help publicly-funded universities and research hospitals identify research with commercial potential, develop innovative new products and forge partnerships with the private sector*" (Industry Canada 2003, emphasis mine). Dr. John Evans, former president of the University of Toronto and Chair of the Board of the new centre, added:

> We are delighted that the provincial and federal governments are both supporting this world-class convergence centre for life science, information technology and other related disciplines. This program will create a close-knit research community that will attract the best and brightest researchers, entrepreneurs, venture capital and professional services. The MaRS Discovery District *will make Ontario and the rest of Canada leaders in the development and commercialization of new technologies*. (Industry Canada 2003, emphasis mine)

The most significant indication of the influence of the expert panel recommendations is the Framework Agreement reached in the Fall of 2002 between the then Minister of Industry, Alan Rock, and the presidents of Canada's universities. According to the press release from Industry Canada, the university presidents committed their universities to doubling the amount of research they perform and tripling their commercialization performance by 2010 (Industry Canada 2002).

To my knowledge, none of the presidents have yet revealed how these targets will be achieved. Moreover, none consulted with the academic senates of their own universities before making these commitments. Finally, no announcements have been made that clarify how commercialization performance will be measured. Nonetheless, the full text of Minister Rock's press statement clearly links increased research productivity and commercialization of research to the massive increase of funds that will have been achieved by 2010 through the CFI and CRC programs. It matters little that the government that was the partner to this agreement has gone out of office because the conservative government under Stephen Harper has been equally if not more aggressive about commercializing university research. In the context of the Framework Agreement, the Expert Panel's recommendations have been a strong inducement to administrations to increase their universities' collaborations with private sector firms in order to convert research discoveries into commercial products. Thinking strategically, they are encouraged to view their faculty members as potential income generators and their research findings as potentially sellable product, thus strengthening and consolidating universities' transformation into knowledge businesses.

Trouble in the University-on-the-Ground

The foregoing discussion tends to present Canadian universities' engagement with public policy as a relatively linear, cumulative development. However, it has not been simple and straightforward to try to install an agenda designed to generate support for private sector innovation and economic development into a public institution that, until recently, has pursued more broadly conceived social purposes. For one thing, the policy has not been even-handed and consistent. For another, different policies from different levels of government have not always cohered. Moreover, initiatives from the same level of government have sometimes conflicted with and even undermined, or threatened to undermine, the initiating government's stated purposes.

In the final section of this chapter, I will briefly touch on some ways that these imbalances, contradictions and incoherencies are playing out in the university-on-the ground. The discussion is by no means comprehensive. The most I can do within the space of this chapter is to name some of the critical tensions in these emerging knowledge businesses. On an optimistic note, these tensions may offer those who oppose this policy direction opportunities for intervention.

Loss of Public Trust

> We know that the universities are in crisis and are attempting to ride out the storm by aligning themselves with various corporate interests. That is short sighted and self-destructive. *From the point of view of their obligation to society, it is simply irresponsible.*" (Saul 1995: 173, emphasis mine)

Citing Dorothy Smith's view that public policies are active forces rather than discrete events, Claire Polster makes this important observation:

> When a policy involves or produces a qualitative break from the past, it is likely to generate a greater number of issues to be addressed and to transform possibilities for strategic intervention to a greater degree than is generally the case. (Polster 2002: 297)

One of the most troubling of the "issues to be addressed" is the loss in public trust arising in large part because, as Saul states, universities have attempted to "ride out the storm by aligning themselves with various corporate interests."

Ironically, this loss in public trust has especially focused on the prestigious University of Toronto (U of T). In June 1998, an investigative article was published on U of T's highly controversial $400 million fundraising campaign carried out under the leadership of then President, Robert

Prichard. Investigative journalist Trevor Cole titled his article "Ivy League Hustle" (Cole 1998).[5] Accordingly, he represents Prichard and the university's chief development officer, Jon Delandrea, as artful dealmakers who mix and match the university's most highly prized programmes and intellectual resources to the particular interests of primarily corporate donors. He asks, "Is Rob Prichard, a man of hand shakes and 'how-are-ya's, more interested in protecting the university's cash than its academic freedoms?" (Cole 1998: 36).

As if to answer this question, within a year the University of Toronto was engulfed by two widely reported international scandals, one involving a family physician and medical researcher, Dr. Nancy Olivieri, and the other involving psycho-pharmacologist David Healy. In the Olivieri case, the university administration refused to back Dr. Olivieri's decision to tell her patients about potential dangers with a drug she was researching under a funding contract with Apotex, the drug's manufacturer. The university administration justified its stand on the grounds that Olivieri, in the early 1990s, had signed a funding contract in which she had agreed to not disclose the results of her research without prior permission from Apotex. The incident took several years to resolve, involving, among other things, several in-house investigations, an international panel of experts to assess Olivieri's research, and two formal inquiries, one undertaken by the Canadian Association of University Teachers which was highly critical of the conduct of the University of Toronto's administration. It also received worldwide coverage as an example of how corporate funding of research can lead to conflicts of interest among the various partners to the contracts and, in the process, endanger the public interest (Shuchman 2005). Olivieri's own account of the incident notes that the same president of the University of Toronto described by Trevor Cole as an artful deal-maker had been angling for a large donation from Apotex and initially refused to back up her stand about disclosing her research results (Olivieri 2007).

In the fall of 2000, David Healy accepted a job offer from the University of Toronto's Centre for Addiction and Mental Health (CAMH). Prior to commencing the position, he was invited to speak to an international conference on psychiatry held at the Centre where he argued that Prozac, a drug manufactured by Eli Lilly, could provoke suicide attempts in users. Healy's position on Prozac and similar psychotropic drugs was a matter of public record and known to people involved in making the job offer. Nonetheless immediately after the lecture, the job offer was withdrawn, inciting a prolonged investigation of whether Eli Lilly and Company, a significant donor to CAMH, had pressured the university into the withdrawal. Although the university president and Centre officials denied that pressure was exerted on them by Eli Lilly and Company, Canadian Association of University

Teachers' (CAUT) representatives who had become involved in the case as a breech of academic freedom argued:

> Whether the pressure came from a pharmaceutical manufacturer, from a University or CAMH official worried about offending a donor, or from administrators at the university and/or CAMH without any serious thought of the pharmaceutical industry, the action appears to be a very serious attack on academic freedom that should not be countenanced by any university in this country. (CAUT 2001)

That university-corporate partnerships pose dangers to academic freedom and the integrity of science was not a new argument. Critics of policies that encourage university-corporate collaboration had voiced concerns for some time about conflicts of interest and undue corporate pressures. In fact, in the United States, several notorious cases in the late 1980s and early 1990s prompted intervention by the U.S. Congress. But particularly noteworthy about the Olivieri and Healy cases is that they focused attention on one of, if not the, most highly respected academic institution in the country, and that they received international attention and provoked strong reactions from prominent professional and scientific organizations.

Cases like these, even if few in number, feed an image of university administrators as untrustworthy, money-grubbing wheeler-dealers whose every action panders to corporate interests. Moreover, distrust extends to the research that universities produce since many new research initiatives are being funded, at least in part, by corporate donors who stand to benefit financially from the knowledge they will produce. In this sense, then, policies supporting commercialization provoke questions about the university's legitimacy. These questions play into a political climate already less supportive toward public funding of universities, hence making universities even more reliant on other sources of funds. Most important, the university's engagement with commercialization deprives Canadians of a source of independent assessment and judgment precisely when scientific and technological developments in many areas require independent evaluation.[6]

Regulating and Overseeing Academic Work

A second troubling issue is that academic activities in the Canadian university-on-the-ground are being more and more regulated and directed by policies and guidelines that limit the scope of their professional authority. Performance indicators have received considerable critical attention in this regard (Polster and Newson 1998). Here I will focus on another significant development, the implementation of a national level ethics regime for overseeing research involving human participants.

As of 2000, all research undertaken in universities by members of the university community must be reviewed and approved by the local institution's research ethics board/committee (REB or REC). REBs are required to apply criteria that define appropriate research conduct as they are specified in the code of ethical conduct developed by the three national research councils.

This form of ethics regulation is distinguished from previous forms in that: (a) it uses the same criteria for all research, whether in professional fields like law, medicine, business, the natural and physical sciences or the social sciences and humanities; (b) it applies to all research undertaken by members of the university community — faculty, staff and students, including undergraduates — whether or not the research is funded; (c) the local process of review is overseen by, and integrated into, a national level ethics regulation structure; and (d) universities that fail to ensure that the protocol is implemented in full are denied access to federal research funds.

This extensive, compulsory system of ethical regulation is justified largely on the grounds that public confidence needs to be restored in universities and their research, especially in light of cases such as Olivieri and Healy as described above. In other words, perversely, these forms of regulation are designed to assure the public that potential threats to their interests will not occur while at the same time the overall policy direction that leads to these threats is being maintained. Ethics reviews under the tri-council policy can be likened to good-house-keeping seals of approval: they certify that certain — but only certain[7] — ethical standards are employed in research undertakings. Featured on university websites, they are part and parcel of the instruments of university-corporate collaboration and necessary for the public-relations campaigns of competitive knowledge businesses (Newson 2009).

Especially troubling for many academic researchers, however, is that the Tri-Council ethics protocol constrains academic and professional judgments about how to conduct their research relationships, even to the extent of limiting their academic freedom to choose research strategies commensurate with their own intellectual, moral and political commitments. Academics who want to engage participants as collaborators rather than as research subjects, as advocated by feminist researchers for example, or who engage in research that focuses on issues that are politically contentious for the organization or community under study are greatly impeded by the requirements of the protocol (Newson 2007; van den Hoonard 2001). In other words, the protocol is not neutral toward the kind of research that is undertaken.

Academic researchers on-the-ground are adopting a variety of strategies to deal with this problem. Some are refraining from research that involves human participants. Some are choosing to refrain from using qualitative methods, instead engaging in quantitative studies that are more compatible with the protocol requirements. Some are discontinuing the practice of involving their undergraduate students in research projects as part of their teaching because securing ethics approval is time consuming and also compels them to teach their students the approach to research ethics that the Tri-Council policy endorses. Some even are engaging in research without submitting an ethics review.

But these strategies are also not neutral in their effects. For example, changing research designs in order to receive ethics approval may mean that academics are more likely to engage inadvertently in research that serves and favours the interests of political and economic elites, or that creates knowledges that are supportive rather than critical of dominant ways of understanding the world (Newson 2007). Moreover, even though this form of ethics regulation is part and parcel of a policy direction premised on the need to promote innovation and cutting edge developments, in practice it limits, rather than encourages, innovative thinking. To develop new knowledges and practical techniques, research designs and strategies that provoke and challenge are required, rather than designs and strategies that reinforce established ways of knowing and acting in the world.

Diminished Teaching and the Rise of the Student-Consumer

A third contradiction and inconsistency in the university-on-the-ground is the balance between the research and teaching functions of universities. There are growing indications that the high priority assigned to research activities does not cohere well with providing high quality undergraduate education.

In *No Place to Learn*, political scientists Tom Pocklington and Alan Tupper are sharply critical of Canada's universities for short-changing undergraduate education while increasing their involvement in specialized areas of research (Tupper and Pocklington 2004). They support this charge by pointing to: (a) the increased use of short-contract lecturers to teach first year and foundational disciplinary courses; (b) large lecture formats for courses; (c) the greater significance assigned in tenure decisions and other decisions that affect a faculty member's career prospects to their research productivity as compared to their teaching performance; and (d) the recruitment of students to graduate programs based on their research potential rather than their teaching potential.

As well as criticizing university administrations and faculty members for prioritizing the research function of universities over their educational function, they also implicate the national research grant councils for encouraging this trend through providing teaching replacement costs as part of research grant awards so full-time tenure stream academics can receive teaching release. Furthermore, they argue, the mutual reinforcement hypothesis — that research enlivens teaching and that good researchers are good teachers and vice versa — has become a myth held on to by university administrators and faculty members in spite of their own contradictory practices. Among their reasons for discrediting the mutual-reinforcement thesis, they cite the priority assigned by the granting councils — which university administrators and researchers accommodate — to highly specialized cutting edge research that does not enhance undergraduate teaching. In a recent commentary, Pocklington states:

> universities equate "research" as one type of research, that which they designate as "frontier" or "cutting edge." This means research that discovers new facts. Research that involves critical examination of widely accepted assumptions, speculation about the connections between apparently diverse phenomena, and reconsideration of aesthetic and moral postulates and political lore — the kind of research that has a bearing on undergraduate teaching — is seen as second rate. (Pocklington 2005)

It is not difficult to relate the experiences and perspectives that Tucker and Pocklington gleaned from their interviews with front-line faculty members to the policies previously discussed. For over a decade, the public funding policies of the federal government have pumped large sums of money into university research while monies from the provincial governments that support university teaching programs and operating budgets have been well below levels required to maintain their quality. Moreover, government spokespersons, high-ranking members of the research councils as well as the written descriptions of and prescriptions for various research grant programs emphasize and priorize research that contributes to wealth-creation, economic innovation and leading edge, commercializable intellectual property. Not surprisingly, administrations' and faculty members' actions on-the-ground have followed the money.

But following the money has created a paradoxical situation for students as well as for university administrators and faculty members: the same policy direction that promotes greater research productivity and commercializing academic research also promotes the idea that, as the individual beneficiaries of their education, students should contribute more to its costs. While university teaching and learning is declining in quality and taking a second seat to research, tuition fees for students attending universities have increased to an unprecedented degree across the country.

I don't have space to discuss all of the domino effects of this contradictory situation. Suffice it to say that many Canadian universities, including my own, are busily trying to advertise their way out of their declining quality of education problems. Students correspondingly adopt an increasingly consumerist orientation toward their education while faculty members respond to students' consumerism with bewilderment, or frustration, or condemnation, or defeat, or neglect or a mix of all of these.

Heather Menzies and I recently conducted a study in which we asked faculty members from across the country about their workload, their ways of managing time, choosing priorities and using online technology in their work (Menzies and Newson 2007, 2008). Many of them commented upon the consumerism of students as not only a major teaching challenge but also one reason that they feel less enthusiastic about teaching. They cited students' aggressive demands that courses be made as easy and convenient as possible — for example, that faculty members post lecture notes on line and respond to their questions through e-mail communication rather than requiring them to attend classes or meet them in their office hours. They reported that students have stated explicitly that the high cost of tuition entitles them to convenient service and even to high grades, sometimes prefacing these demands with phrases like, "my tuition pays your salary" or " I pay enough for this course and you should make sure that I know what I need to know to get a good grade" or "I shouldn't be required to shut off my cell phone in class."

To be sure, comments like these do not come from the majority of students. Nevertheless they reveal a growing and not uncommon orientation among students that matches the increasingly corporate culture of universities. Students regard themselves, and are regarded by universities, as customers who pay for a service and who therefore have the right to make demands that the product they receive will serve their particular purposes well.

Compounding the situation is the increasing reliance on student course evaluations to assess teaching performance not only for tenure and career-related decisions that affect faculty members individually, but also for measuring the status of departments, faculties and whole institutions vis-à-vis other institutions. In order to avoid poor performance evaluations, faculty members as well as administrators anticipate, and through advertising, try to influence, students' consumerist concerns, either to accommodate them or to avoid imposing conditions and requirements that might lead to complaints and dissatisfaction. Students' consumerism thus exerts a growing influence on the pedagogical and curricular decisions that both faculty members and university administrations make. In the study I conducted with Menzies, some respondents indicated that they felt as though the traditional student-teacher relationship is being reversed, with student preferences exercising greater influence over pedagogy than the intellectual judgment and concerns of faculty members. Moreover, the legalistic student rights framework adopted by university administrations encourages students to appropriate the consumer model as the only legitimate means for influencing the university, as customers rather than citizens or members of an intellectual community (Brulé 2004).

Canadian economists such as David Laidler, Lorne Carmichael and

John Chant of the University of Western Ontario, Queens University, and Simon Fraser University respectively, advocate funding policies that build upon, rather than seek to diminish, students' power as consumers of education. They argue that their proposals will help to ameliorate the problem of declining quality of education while also being equitable and fair.

Laidler, for example, acknowledges that recent initiatives in government funding policy have encouraged universities to allocate their resources to applied and results-oriented research, interdisciplinarity and serving a corporatist agenda. These priorities involve high overhead and maintenance budgets, drawing resources away from other areas of activity and encouraging administrations to use areas such as the humanities and social sciences as cash cows that operate at lower academic standards. Therefore, he argues,

> Allowing tuition revenue to become the main source of universities' income would allow students to seek out good quality academic programs and universities to compete more directly to offer such programs as a counterweight to current reliance on government and business sectors in setting universities' priorities. Allowing fees for different programs to better reflect actual program costs while allowing students to choose among these differently priced programs would end up allocating resources within universities efficiently without the need for central or ministry direction. This would also foster greater differentiation and specialization across different universities with students playing a significant role in this resource-allocation process.[8]

Chant takes the argument a step further. He proposes that governments should not fund institutions at all but rather fund only students, thus eliminating what he views to be the central problem of Canadian higher education, that it is too highly directed and overly regulated (Chant 2005: 587).

These proposals rest on assumptions that can be challenged in several ways. For example, enhancing students' leverage as consumers in no way ensures that educational quality will increase, since one cannot assume that student applicants have direct or reliable knowledge of the factors that are relevant to higher educational quality and even if they did, that these factors would be the reason for their choices. However, I have raised these proposals to illustrate that, even though Laidler and Chant criticize and seek to redress certain aspects of higher education policy in Canada, they frame both the problems and their proposals within the context of the university-as-knowledge-business engaged in the competition for resources, responsive to external, especially economic, pressures and infinitely flexible in supplying whatever programs and services are in demand. If adopted, these policies will drive universities even farther along that path of development.

Creative Time and Production Pressures

Perhaps the most troubling of the concerns arising from the cacophonous interplay of recent policy initiatives is one that strikes at the heart of the university's *raison d'etre*, that it is one of society's main repositories of intellectual creativity and critical reflection.

On the one hand, the policy direction traced in previous sections of this paper is justified on grounds that it will enable universities to engage in innovative, cutting edge knowledge quests for the benefit of Canadian society as a whole. Words such as creative, world class, excellence and path breaking are often embedded in the rhetoric that promotes these policies, and in university academic plans and mission statements that claim to respond to them. On the other hand, academics themselves frequently report that conditions in the university-on-the-ground are hardly conducive to creative scholarship and reflective thinking.

For one thing, many argue that the university is now being expected to do too many things, often without adequate resources. Faculty members as a consequence are pulled in too many directions. For example, more and more they are expected to compete for the substantial grants that are available to support research initiatives, including developing partnerships with potential funders and when successful, managing the organizational and reporting requirements of often very large sums of money. As well, the change in students' orientation as described above often pressures faculty members into providing students with online assistance at all hours of the day and week, and to prepare lecture materials and other supportive documents for online posting. Cost-cutting, computerization and online systems of reporting have transferred to faculty members many of the tasks that were once carried out by support staff. Moreover, administrations have chosen or are pressed by limited funds to serve increasing numbers of students through using short-term and part-time contract teaching positions. Thus the responsibility for program development and day-to-day functioning of departments and faculties falls disproportionately on reduced numbers of full-time, tenure track, faculty members.

Added to these increased expectations on faculty members individually are the increased production pressures on the university as a whole. As described previously, universities compete with each other to retain their rankings and eligibility for shares of research funds. In the 2002 Framework Agreement, presidents of universities agreed to double their university's research productivity and triple their commercializable research performance. Hence, pressures increase on faculty members to engage in this productive research, to pursue commercialization opportunities while being inundated with reporting requirements to enhance their university's production record.

Arguably, these intense and diverse demands on faculty members' time and energy squeeze out the reflective time and focus needed for creative work. The study that I conducted with Heather Menzies provided evidence to this effect: regardless of discipline, career stage or gender, the overwhelming majority of respondents indicated that they had less time than in earlier stages of their career for reflective and creative thinking and that their reading and knowledge of scholarly literature was narrower and more specialized than it used to be or than they liked it to be. Many affirmed that their current working conditions militate against the creative and reflective thought that they associate with scholarship. The previously mentioned study by Tom Pocklington and Alan Tupper adds witness to this situation. Pocklington reports that in their interviews with Canadian faculty members from across the country, several science and technology professors told them that "there is an almost irresistible temptation to publish a stream of short, partial, episodic papers instead of occasional, broad and deep ones" (Pocklington 2005).

Advocates of the new policy direction would probably argue that these manifestations of contradictory and conflicting pressures created by universities' attempts to respond to recent policy initiatives are temporary. They might say that the current cohort of university faculty are unaccustomed to new ways of doing science, working with industry and delivering educational services to specific markets; and that after a period of adjustment and faculty turnover, a new, more innovative and entrepreneurial breed of academics will emerge to take advantage of the new opportunities made available through these policies.

However, even if time for adjustment is given and the current generation of academics is replaced, a fundamental issue remains: does the pursuit of creative and innovative intellectual work cohere with the objectives, timetables and methodologies of industry? The early advocates of this policy direction, such as Judith Maxwell and Stephanie Currie, argued that academics are overly attached to an academic culture that is too isolated and out of step with the needs of progressive, knowledge-based societies: they need to let go of cherished traditions such as academic freedom and scientific autonomy in order for knowledge to progress. Others have argued that, through care and persistence, corporate and academic culture will merge into a new mode of knowledge production that will bring benefits to universities, corporations and society as a whole (Gibbons et al. 1994).

By contrast, Dutch social theorist Dik Pels argues that institutional frameworks that are suitable to conducting business, politics and media relations do not match with the kind of time, uses of time and modes of communication required for scientific thought to advance. He identifies the external pressures of enterprise culture, performance-based measurements, media publicity and the spread into academe of the cult of celebrity as factors that rush scientific thinking and discovery to the point where it threatens to lose its special-ness and hence its value to society. Science, says Pels, requires deceleration and un-hastening to distinguish it from faster-paced cultures associated with politics, economic management and journalism. He argues:

> Surely, the primary condition for a successful working of the "logic of scientific discovery" is absence of haste, or a systematic and critical deceleration of thought and action which sets science apart from the demands of urgency, immediacy, simultaneity, and publicity which are imposed by more "speedy" practices. This gesture of *un-hastening* the ever-increasing velocity of everyday life and professional cultures, which aims to unravel and reduce their astounding complexity, immediately goes with the pragmatic requisite of clearing a relatively bounded space, within which intellectuals and scientists can be rigorously selective about their topics and legitimately ignore the plethora of other issues that might clamour for their attention. This selectivity enables them to "freeze frame," take things apart, focus on tiny details, and leisurely ponder on their broader significance; to slow down conversations and conflicts by means of quiet turn-takings and long communicative intervals (e.g. reading and writing rather than talking face-to-face); and more generally, to postpone decisions about what the world is like and what one should do about it. (Pels 2005: 221)

It remains to be seen, of course, whether the oil and water mix of academic, business, political and public relations interests will produce the innovative and creative breakthroughs in knowledge that advocates of current policy have anticipated. However, I am convinced that one of the most pressing priorities of our time is that space and time for reflective, evaluative critical thinking and even more so for cultivating the capacities and sensibilities to sustain it are basic requirements. If the university fails to address *this* urgent societal need, then the knowledges and know-how that it produces may no longer feed the soul or nurture reasoned, ethical stances as the basis for intervening in world affairs. Other spaces for doing this will have to be found.

A Concluding Statement

I have traced a path of development in Canadian universities over the past three decades and identified several troubling issues that arise in the university-on-the-ground for administrators, faculty members, staff and students trying to respond to the policy initiatives that have engaged the university on its current trajectory.

Similar developments have unfolded in universities in other national contexts. Some scholars attribute this apparent convergence in university development across the globe to the influence of postmodernism, neoliberalism or third-wayism (Delanty 2003). Neoliberalism has been especially influential in accounts of changes in systems of higher education, as anyone will find out if they browse through academic journals on higher education and social theory issued over the last decade or more.

I believe that there is value in collecting together various aspects of university transformation and relating them to an over-arching theoretical framework or to broad- based political-economic forces and dominant discourses, as long as analysts are careful to explore how the manifestations of such phenomena vary under the specifics of local conditions. Even so, I have tended to resist doing this in my own work. On the one hand, over-arching theoretical accounts sometimes obscure the particular processes by which social and cultural transformations take place: the details are too often seen through the lens of the theory and are not allowed space to speak for themselves before they are assimilated into the theory. On the other hand, I have wanted to challenge the common assumption that there is a direct line between government policies and their implementation by universities and their constituencies. In writings on higher education, frequently one finds statements such as "higher education has been invaded by neoliberalism" or "the university has succumbed to postmodernism" or "governments are privatizing universities and colleges" as though external political and economic forces are able to mechanically transform complex institutions like universities without the mediation of diverse internal social actors.

Equally important, terms like succumbing and invading leave little room for intervention because they don't reveal the agents of change; in fact, they hide the fact that there are agents. By contrast, making visible the role of various actors in mediating policy initiatives is of great value intellectually and practically. It enables us to see that and how policies advance a particular conception of the university in the service of nameable political, economic and cultural interests. It also reveals the ways in which policies are agented by more than governments and sometimes originate in some form within the academy, through proposals designed by scholars who are themselves wedded to particular intellectual and professional orientations, discourses and ideologies. Equally important, it exposes points of leverage where interventions can be made to subvert, challenge or even transform the apparent objectives of policies.

But perhaps the most important conclusion to draw is that the university and its members are implicated in their own transformation as well as in the transformation of society and the world at large. The academic community is not innocent nor a passive victim of external actors. Using neoliberalism as the example here because of its contemporary currency in critical higher education scholarship, I think it would be intellectually fruitful to consider the ways in which neoliberalism or at least policies and policy discourses that seek to implement it have in turn been shaped by the university's complex engagements with them. Without being able to defend it well at this point – offering it more as a discussion point than a definitive position — I want to propose that neoliberalism should not be understood as a way of thinking from nowhere. Over the twenty-five years or so of its ascendancy, the social and cultural institutions and locales to which its ideas and policies have been applied — and the social actors engaged within them— have in turn shaped neoliberalism. We who seek to better understand the world in which our universities are currently functioning may benefit from this realization.

Notes

1. A version of this chapter with a different introduction and conclusion was published in the June 2006 *Puerto Rico Higher Education Research and Information Center Journal*, Inaugural Edition (online). The then editor recently confirmed that this journal published only one issue and now no longer exists because the Puerto Rican Higher Education Council that housed the journal was partly disbanded and merged into a comprehensive Education Council. It is truly regrettable that the work of the editor and other academic colleagues has been diminished in this way. They gave much energy to creating and raising funds for the seminar to which I and other speakers were invited, as well as to creating a scholarly journal, in order to include Puerto Rican scholarship on higher education in international discussions.

2. Claire Polster coined the term "knowledge business."

3. The organization consisted of twenty-five Canadian university presidents and twenty-five leading Canadian business executives. It was a counterpart to the Business-Higher Education Forum established in the U.S. in 1979.

4. Throughout the 1980s, published critiques of this new policy direction for universities were few: in fact, many higher education scholars were either reluctant to publicly express their position on this matter or they tended to downplay the significance of the policy changes that were being enacted. In addition to my own work, my collaborations with Howard Buchbinder, Paul Axelrod, Marguerite Cassin, E. Margaret Conrad, Len Findlay, Ursula Franklin, William Graham, Michael Katz, Graham Morgan, Blair Neatby, Neil Tudiver and Howard Woodhouse are among the few I recall who, early on, publicly criticized these policies.

5. Interestingly, Cole's article was followed in March 2000 by a similar article about corporate collaborations undertaken by leading U.S. research universities written by Eyal Press and Jennifer Washburn with an equally provocative title, "The Kept University."

6. The recent controversy over COX-2 inhibitors like Celebrex and Vioxx is a case in point. Both the FDA in the U.S. and Health Canada have been criticized for too quickly approving these drugs and some groups have called for a source of assessments that is independent from either government or corporate influence.

No more than three decades ago, the university would have been trusted as such a source.

7. The Tri-Council criteria apply to researchers' relationships with their participants — they do not address issues related to the interests of funders, the content of contracts signed with funders and the possible uses of the research.

8. I am quoting from Laidler's summary found at <jdi.econ.queensu.ca/ Publications/HigherEducation.html> of his article published in Charles M. Beach, Robin W. Boadway and R. Marvin McInnis (eds.), 2005, *Higher Education in Canada*. Kingston, Ontario: Queens University.

References

Berkowitz, Peggy. 1999. "Panel Softens Stance on Commercializing IP." *University Affairs* (June/July).

Brulé, Elisabeth. 2004. "Going to Market: Neo-liberalism and the Social Construction of the University Student as an Autonomous Consumer." In Marilee Reimer (ed.), *Gender and the Corporate University*. Toronto: Sumach Press.

Buchbinder, Howard, and Janice Newson. 1990. "Corporate-University Linkages in Canada: Transforming a Public Institution." *Higher Education* 20.

Canadian Association of University Teachers. 2001. "Academic Freedom in Jeopardy at Toronto." *CAUT Bulletin* (May).

Chan, Adrienne, and Donald Fisher (eds.). 2008. *The Exchange University: Corporatization of Academic Culture*. Vancouver: University of British Columbia Press.

Chant, John. 2005. "University Accountability." In Charles M. Beach, Robin W. Boadway and R. Marvin McInnis (eds.), *Higher Education in Canada*. Kingston: Queens University.

Cole, Trevor. 1998. "Ivy League Hustle." *Report on Business Magazine* (June).

Delanty, Gerard. 2003. "Ideologies of the Knowledge Society and the Cultural Contradictions of Higher Education." *Policy Futures in Education* 1, 1.

Enros, Philip, and Michael Farley. 1986. *University Offices For Technology Transfer: Toward the Service University*. Ottawa: Science Council of Canada.

Fisher, Donald, and Kjell Rubenson. 1998. "The Changing Political Economy: The Private and Public Lives of Canadian Universities." In Jan Currie and Janice Newson (eds.), *Universities and Globalisation: Critical Perspectives*. Thousand Oaks: Sage Publications.

Gibbons, Michael Camille Limoges, Helga Nowotny, Simon Schwartzman, Peter Scott, and Martin Trow. 1994. *The New Production of Knowledge*. Thousand Oaks: Sage Publications.

Hardy, Cynthia. 1996. *The Politics of Collegiality: Retrenchment Strategies in Canadian Universities*. Montréal: McGill-Queens University Press.

Industry Canada. 2003. Press Release, April 22. Industry Canada email list-serv.

___. 2002. Press Release, November 22. Industry Canada email list-serv.

Keller, George. 1983. *Academic Strategy: The Management Revolution in Higher Education*. Baltimore: Johns Hopkins University Press.

Maxwell, Judith, and Stephanie Currie. 1984. *Partnership for Growth*. Montréal: Corporate-Higher Education Forum.

Menzies, Heather, and Janice Newson. 2008. "Time, Stress and Intellectual

Engagement in Academic Work: Exploring the Gender Difference." *Gender Work and Organisation* 15, 5 (Special Issue).

____. 2007. "No Time to Think: Academics in the Globally Wired University." *Time & Society* 16, 1.

National Sciences and Engineering Research of Canada. 1999. "Backgrounder: Summary of the Expert Panel's Report." At <nserc.ca/news/1999/p990830. htm>.

Newson, Janice. 2009. "Re-Making the Space for Professional Response-Ability: Lessons From the Corporate-Linked University." In Graham Owen (ed.), *Architecture, Ethics and Globalization*. New York: Routledge.

____. 2007. "Ethics Regimes and the Commercialization of Academic Research." *Apuesta* 2.

____. 2004. "Disrupting the Student-Consumer Model." *International Studies* 18, 2.

____. 1998. "The Corporate Linked University: From Social Project to Market Force." *Canadian Journal of Communication* 23 (Special Issue).

____. 1996. "Positioning the Social Sciences and Economic Re-structuring." Presidential Address to the Canadian Sociology and Anthropology Association, Université du Québec a Montréal, Montréal, June 1995. Published in *Society/ Société*.

____. 1992. "The Decline of Faculty Influence: Confronting the Corporate Agenda." In William Carroll *et al.* (eds.), *Fragile Truths: Twenty-Five Years of Sociology and Anthropology in Canada*. Ottawa: Carleton University Press.

Newson, Janice, and Howard Buchbinder. 1988. *The University Means Business: Universities, Corporations, and Academic Work*. Toronto: Garamond Press.

Olivieri, Nancy. 2000. "When Money and Truth Collide." In James Turk (ed.), *The Corporate Campus: Commercialization and the Dangers to Canada's Colleges and Universities*. Toronto: James Lorimer and Company.

Pels, Dik. 2003. "Un-hastening Science." *European Journal of Social Theory* 6, 2.

Pocklington, Tom. 2005. "Why Universities Aren't Working." *Express News*, April 25. At <expressnews.ualberta.ca/article.cfm?id=2684>.

____. 2002. "A Break From the Past: Impacts and Implications of the Canada Foundation for Innovation and the Canada Research Chairs Initiative." *Canadian Review of Sociology and Anthropology* 39, 3.

____. 1998. "From Public Resource to Industry's Instrument: Redefining and Reshaping the Production of Knowledge in Canada's Universities." *Canadian Journal of Communication* 23, 1.

____. 1996. "Dismantling the Liberal University: The State's New Approach to Academic Research." In Bob Brecher *et al.* (eds.), *The University in a Liberal State*. Ashford: Avebury Press.

Pocklington, Tom, and Alan Tupper. 2004. *No Place To Learn*. Vancouver: University of British Columbia Press.

Polster, Claire. 1994. "Compromising Positions: The Federal Government and the Reorganization of the Social Relations of Canadian Academic Research." Unpublished doctoral thesis, York University.

Polster, Claire, and Janice Newson. 1998. "Don't Count Your Blessings: The Social Accomplishments of Performance Indicators." In Jan Currie and Janice Newson (eds.), *The University and Globalisation: Critical Perspectives*. Thousand Oaks: Sage

Publications.

Press, Eyal, and Jennifer Washburn. 2000. "The Kept University." *The Atlantic Monthly* (March): 39–54.

Saul, John Ralston. 1995. *The Unconscious Civilization: The 1995 Massey Lectures.* Toronto: Anansi Press.

Shuchman, Miriam. 2005. *The Drug Trial: Nancy Olivieri and the Science Scandal that Rocked the Hospital for Sick Children.* Toronto: Random House.

Smith, Dorothy. 2010. "A Career Against The Grain." In Janice Newson and Claire Polster (eds.), *Academic Callings: The University We Have Had, Now Have, and Could Have.* Toronto: Canadian Scholars Press.

Tri-Council. 1996. *Tri-Council Policy Statement: Code of Conduct for Research Involving Humans.* Ottawa: Medical Research Council of Canada, Natural Sciences and Engineering Research Council of Canada, Social Sciences and Humanities Research Council of Canada.

Tudiver, Neil. 1999. *Universities for Sale: Resisting Corporate Control over Canadian Higher Education.* Toronto: James Lorimer.

Turk, James (ed.). 2000. *The Corporate Campus: Commercialization and the Dangers to Canada's Colleges and Universities.* Toronto: James Lorimer.

van den Hoonaard, Will. 2001. "Is Research-Ethics a Moral Panic?" *Canadian Review of Sociology and Anthropology* 38, 1.

Woodhouse, Howard. 2009. *Selling Out: Academic Freedom and the Corporate Market.* Montréal: McGill-Queens University Press.

Zinberg, S. Dorothy. 1990. *The Changing University: How Increased Demand for Scientists and Technology Is Transforming Academic Institutions Internationally.* Boston: Kluwer Academic Publishers.

Part Three

FEMINISM AND THE ACADEMY: REMEMBERING HISTORY/ RECALLING RESISTANCE

Chapter Six

BLUESTOCKINGS AND GODDESSES
Writing Feminist Cultural History

Ann Shteir

Working to reconsider feminist knowledge, what can feminist scholars learn from studying female celebrities and icons in earlier centuries? What resources can help us craft knowledge for feminist cultural history that is thick and layered and that acknowledges the complexities of individual lives and stories? This chapter is meant as a challenge to women's studies to take the past more seriously as an element in scholarship and activism in our time. Based in my own work on women, gender and science and on women in cultures of knowledge over the past several centuries, I present a mini-panorama from eighteenth-century England of one group of women intellectuals, two artistic and literary women and two goddesses from Roman mythology that were widely invoked as symbols of female identity. The group is the cultural phenomenon known as the "Bluestockings." One of their members was Elizabeth Carter (1717–1806), celebrated as England's preeminent female intellectual. Linked to that circle was Angelica Kauffman (1741–1807), a professional artist famous across Europe for her portraits and history paintings of classical subjects. In the visual culture of that time, mythology from Ancient Greece and Rome was part of cultural and gendered vocabularies, and Elizabeth Carter and Angelica Kauffman both were represented with reference to Minerva, the goddess of wisdom, learning and the arts in Roman mythology. Flora, the goddess of flowers, was also part of the visual and textual lexicon that came to eighteenth-century England from Roman mythology.

Elizabeth Carter and Angelica Kauffman lived in actual time and place. Minerva and Flora have lived in the cultural imaginary and carried considerable freight over many centuries. All these female figures — the real women and the symbolic ones — were part of the gender economies of their day, and performed dynamic allegorical, symbolic and socio-cultural work. In our time, when attention to intersectionalities in feminist studies has generated so many new questions and new findings about female identity and the tensions and shaping forces in women's lives, I believe that adding historical perspectives will make feminist analysis and activism even more productive. Knowledge of mythology is one particular tool that I highlight here for purposes of feminist cultural history.

Restoring Bluestockings

In the mid-1700s, a group of friends, both female and male, began meeting in London and a few other places for literary and intellectually improving conversation. They got together in informal and domestic settings, usually in the late afternoon, hosted by several wealthy English women who wanted to cultivate intellectual community. They came to be known by the collective name "Bluestockings" because one of the participants, the scholar and botanist Benjamin Stillingfleet, wore informal worsted blue hosiery to their meetings rather than the white silk stockings expected for court or ceremonial occasions. Before long, the term "Bluestockings" came to refer to women. The "Blues," as they also were known, exemplified intellectual women in their time. During the decades from the 1750s through the 1780s, the Bluestockings were celebrated for their achievements in literature, philosophy, history and the arts. We, however, have forgotten them, and they are largely erased from feminist cultural histories. Over the past decades, postmodern and postcolonial scholars have critiqued the Age of Enlightenment for Eurocentric, universalizing beliefs and for scientism and commitment to ideas about objectivity. I take a more historicized and humanist position on the spirit and practice of the European Enlightenment as a time when foundational thinkers in Europe across the long eighteenth century — John Locke, Voltaire, Denis Diderot and Mary Wollstonecraft, to name a few — celebrated the human capacity to reason and pursue knowledge both systematically and collaboratively as pathways to improvement for individuals and collectivities of many kinds. Many publications from that period took the form of dialogues, for example, because the exchange of ideas within groups was greatly valued. Exemplifying Enlightenment beliefs, Bluestocking circles were imbued with high-mindedness. They provided a forum for good conversation and sociability among writers, artists, intellectuals and other figures of culture. The Bluestockings modeled their vision of intellectual community on that of the French salons, but with a greater orientation toward the middle classes and gentry rather than the world of the aristocracy and court.

As the eighteenth century went along, the term "bluestocking" became generalized to a woman who pursued the life of the mind, often with autonomy and a sense of profession, as learned women, professional artists and active and deliberate published writers. The Blues represented modernity and forward-looking values of culture and intellectual exchange, and that is how they were depicted in a painting from 1778 entitled "Portraits in the Characters of the Muses in the Temple of Apollo (The Nine Living Muses of Great Britain)" (see figure 1). The artist, Richard Samuel, pays tribute there to women who were active in the artistic, literary and intellectual culture of that time. His intention was to demonstrate the progress of civil society and give a boost to the national pride of Great Britain by depicting a female

Republic of Letters inhabited by novelists, poets, playwrights, singers and others, most of whom were professionals earning a living from their work. The figures in the Samuel portrait look undifferentiated and are idealized, but an earlier version of this image, circulated within print culture, made clear who was who. Elizabeth Carter is shown standing in profile at the top left of the composition. Angelica Kauffmann sits at a large painter's easel on that same side, posed in front of her canvas, and gazing with a painter's eye at other muses assembled in the Bluestocking circle. The other "Living Muses" are Anna Letitia Barbauld, Elizabeth Sheridan, Charlotte Lennox, Hannah More, Elizabeth Montague, Elizabeth Griffith and Catharine Macaulay. It may seem discordant to us that the muses portrayed here are such active women, living in the present and working in public and professional endeavours.

Often we think of muses as figures who inspire creativity in others rather than embodying creativity themselves; this representation of passivity is a legacy of Romantic attitudes. In classical Greek culture, by contrast, the Muses were symbolic but active figures of culture. Traditionally nine in number, they personified epic, lyric and sacred poetry (Calliope, Erato, Polyhymnia), history (Clio), music and dance (Euterpe, Terpsichore), comedy and tragedy (Thalia, Melpomene) and astronomy (Urania). In the eighteenth century, Muses were likewise active shapers of culture. Samuel portrays his "Living Muses of Great Britain" as real historical personages, figures of female achievement and emblems of national pride with a sense of group identity. Their visibility in the public culture of their day was so great that visitors to the 1779 summer exhibition at the Royal Academy in London where this painting was on display would have recognized each of the nine women depicted (Eger 2010: 32–58; Peltz 2008: 60–62).

Within too few decades, however, the term bluestocking took on pejorative meanings as Enlightenment ideas were supplanted in a gender backlash associated with the cultural movement of Romanticism. The bluestocking came to be figured less as a female thinker, writer and luminary and more as a pedantic spinster or slovenly bad mother too busy "scribbling" to fulfill her domestic responsibilities. Echoing older satires and denigration of learned women, scientific ladies, and female virtuosi as monstrous, unnatural and mad, the negative vision of a bluestocking prevailed right across the nineteenth century. As a result, acquaintance with the historically specific group in later eighteenth-century England has gone from even a general feminist knowledge base, with a few exceptions. In *A Room of One's Own* (1928) Virginia Woolf celebrates the "activity of mind" and literary labour of bluestocking women in England, but the main point for her is that "women could make money by writing" (Woolf 1975: 65). There was an echo of their politically historical significance in the American radical feminist group Redstockings from the late 1960s and early 1970s, whose "Redstocking Manifesto" called for developing "female class consciousness through sharing experience and publicly exposing the sexist foundation of all our institutions" (cited Crow 2000: 224). The critical dimension of the Bluestocking legacy continues to this day in Bluestockings Bookstore, located on the Lower East Side of New York City. Established in 1999 as a radical bookstore, women's collective and centre for feminist activism, it is now a center for global justice that, according to their Mission Statement, "actively support[s] movements that challenge hierarchy and all systems of oppression" (Bluestocking Bookstore, n.d.). For the most part, the term bluestocking has largely disappeared as a laudatory way to designate intellectual women. Recently, however, feminist philosopher Michèle Le Doeuff has sought, in *The Sex of Knowing* (2003), to revive the legacy of the Bluestocking. Her book is a historical and critical epistemological study of women's access to knowledge that aims to reanimate the power of women who "like to read or think, and do not hide the fact" (Le Doeuff 2003: 2).

Even in the midst of eighteenth-century exultation about the power of

Figure 1 – Richard Samuel, "Portraits in the Characters of the Muses in the Temple of Apollo: The Nine Living Muses of Great Britain" (1778) National Portrait Gallery, London (NPG 4905)

a female Republic of Letters, it was not easy to live as a female intellectual, artist or writer. We would be right to expect gaps between the idealization shown in the Samuel group portrait and the lived reality of the individual women portrayed there. Education was a much-prized Enlightenment route to progress, but was there really an Enlightenment for women? This has been widely debated, as illustrated in the wide-ranging collaborative volume *Women, Gender and Enlightenment*, edited by Sarah Knott and Barbara Taylor in 2005. More women across a broader class range had access to literacy and learning during the eighteenth century than in earlier times, but circumstances of access were limited by class, gender, race and geography. Normative values were in place about women's orderly conduct at various life stages, and sexualized ideas about virtue and reputation still mattered. Across the board, women were praised more for piety, domesticity and constraint than for intellectual brilliance or accomplishment.

So, how did intellectual women deal with the tensions and contradictions of gendered norms and Enlightenment ideals? Two women figured in the Samuel group portrait illustrate opportunities, challenges and strategies. Each a cultural icon of her time, their representations and self-representations are particular to their time and place yet also resonate in early twenty-first century realities.

Elizabeth Carter

Bluestocking Elizabeth Carter (1717–1806) was a classical scholar, poet and translator whose publications included treatises and philosophical work from French, Italian and Greek. She was the daughter of an Anglican clergyman who had progressive Enlightenment views about educating his children, especially in languages and literatures. Early on, she made a commitment to having a professional literary career. After living and working for a while in the London literary world, she left the metropole and joined a family household elsewhere as her way to pursue a life of study. Carter chose not to marry. She also chose to seek financial independence. For ten years she worked on a translation from Greek of philosophical writings by the pre-Christian Stoic thinker Epictetus, whose views she admired on virtue and living a life that is moral and balanced. Publication of *All the Works of Epictetus* by subscription in 1758 brought in real profit for her. Elizabeth Carter was active in Bluestocking circles, and was known for her attachment to friends. In a recent anthology meant to give new readers access to work by eighteenth- and nineteenth-century intellectual women in Britain, Felicia Gordon and Gina Luria Walker write that Elizabeth Carter was by the 1780s "virtually a national institution, renowned for her affability, piety, and philanthropy, attributes that made her scholarship seem palatable to a society sometimes distrustful of female intellect" (Gordon and Walker 2008: 254).

The story of Elizabeth Carter as the preeminent intellectual woman of eighteenth-century England involves both how she was represented and how she represented and fashioned herself. Carter made strategic decisions that took account of her personality and interests and also of gendered and classed parameters of her day. She herself wrote a witty poem entitled "The Dialogue" about the binary between body and mind, set in the form of a dialogue (Carter 1989: 168). The first word goes to Body:

Figure 2 – John Fayram, "Elizabeth Carter as Minerva" (late 1730s) Private ownership but reproduced in *Brilliant Women: Eighteenth-Century Bluestockings*, London: National Portrait Gallery, 2008, p. 72.

Says Body to Mind, "'Tis amazing to see,
We're so nearly related yet never agree,
But lead a most wrangling strange sort of life,
As great plagues to each other as husband and wife." (ll. 1–4)

Mind complains about being "cramped and confined like a slave in a chain" (l. 22) and "shut... in caverns as dark as the night" (l. 28). Body has complaints in turn, but the last word goes to Mind, who is confident about getting rid of Body's "insolent power" (l. 34) and transcending the Body. Mind celebrates this transcendence: "while in the dust your dull ruins decay,/ I'll snap off my chains and fly freely away" (ll. 37–8). An aspiring female intellectual could hardly do otherwise in mid-eighteenth-century England than to stand on the side of the Mind rather than the Body. The portrait "Elizabeth Carter as Minerva," painted by John Fayram, and dating from the later 1730s, is a good diagnostic illustration of this (see figure 2). Painted sometime in the later 1730s when Carter was still a young woman, the portrait was discovered recently in a private collection by curators of the National Portrait Gallery in London, and formed part of a major exhibition of Bluestocking women there in 2008.

Why portray Elizabeth Carter as Minerva? Roman Minerva is Greek Pallas Athena, the goddess of wisdom, learning and the arts and also the goddess of just wars. She is the guardian of civilization, and represents mind and knowledge, rationality and intellect. Minerva is also a virgin goddess, and her chastity is another defining feature of her character, roles and responsibilities as a powerful female figure in mythology. Fayram's portrait shows Elizabeth Carter dressed in armour and a helmet, both of which are traditional attributes associated with Minerva. The emblem on her chest shows the head of the female monster Medusa, whose gaze, it was said, turns enemies to stone; this was based in the classical Greek mythological tale in which the hero Perseus kills the monster with help from Athena and Hermes, and gives the head of Medusa to Athena. The notable departure in Fayram's portrait from a conventional iconography of Minerva is that Elizabeth Carter holds a volume of writings by Plato in her hand rather than a warrior's spear.

Mythology and iconography are excellent resources for feminist cultural history, though still relatively unused as diagnostic and interpretive tools outside art history. Culturally and historically imbued pictorial codes that surround Minerva and other mythological and allegorical figures give complexity to these images. Recent scholarship on allegory and mythology that draws on feminist thinking about embodiment, for example, has opened new ways of thinking. The editors of one current collection of essays about bodies as sites of cultural meaning in early modern visual culture make the point that allegories "operate within the dense network of cultural codes in which both actual and represented bodies become sexed, classed, racially defined and rendered desirable or repellent, safe or dangerous, kin or foreign (Baskins and Rosenthal 2007: 4). Scholarship of this kind challenges us to unpack cultural traffic around images that convey meanings and values, often unwittingly, as though natural and intrinsic.

During the eighteenth century, artists, writers, scholars, skeptics and critics, translators and teachers told and retold, adapted and reshaped stories from Greek and Roman mythology. Some mythographers used their retellings to connect the present to the past so as to justify contemporary social codes and practices. Myths of this kind can have a structuralist "charter" function, for example, that aims, to shore up hierarchies and confirm gender systems (Doherty 2001: 102–26). Others sought to undercut earlier versions of stories, as when Enlightenment skeptics read myths from Greece and Rome as historical record rather than as divinely ordained truths; their accounts put gods and goddesses into mortal forms as historical individuals who were deified to suit politics or nation-building. Among these, the rationalist mythographer Abbé Antoine Banier, for example, wrote a learned and historical cross-cultural study in the 1730s that aimed "to clear the Fable of all that appears in it supernatural, all that pompous Apparatus of Fictions" (Banier 1976: I, 27; Feldman and Richardson 1972: 86–92).

In that same decade, Elizabeth Carter was still a young woman when John Fayram portrayed her as Minerva. His painterly exercise in mythography sets a high threshold for her as a symbol and as a woman inhabiting that symbol. The portrait positions her, and with admiration, as an intellectual woman, but also as a woman taking on a public identity that involved putting herself into body armor and being a warrior for the values that Minerva represented. Going public in this way and in her world, Elizabeth Carter had to look virtuous and also be seen to be that way. She had to cultivate her reality — or at least an appearance of that reality — to fulfill the image. Banier's "Apparatus of Fictions" serves the painter's aspirations by connecting Carter to a goddess from classical antiquity, and buttressed Carter's own aspirations as well.

It should not surprise us to learn about tensions in Elizabeth Carter's story between image and realities, and to wonder about the personal costs of her choices. Carter was a life-long sufferer from migraine headaches and also subject to depression. Her letters include references to her symptoms and their effect on her daily activities. In part to manage her headaches, she developed a regimen of regular and strenuous physical activity. Carter managed her health by walking miles every day and in all weather; a distance of seventeen miles was commonplace for her. "Exercise," Carter wrote to one of her closest Bluestocking correspondents, "is the best remedy and preservative

I know" (cited Blathwayt 2002: 240). Recent feminist scholarship looking to reconsider the Bluestockings has given attention to Bluestocking corporeality and desire, including to what Susan Lanser has termed Bluestocking sapphism. Based in her study of Elizabeth Carter's letters and friendships, Lanser finds passions and energies in Carter that do not fit the Bluestocking image of constraint and self-discipline. This leads her to wonder whether the proprieties in Bluestocking conduct are "'a compensatory conservatism' for managing not only intellectual interests but erotic and affectional interests as well… true Blue might itself [she writes] be a little bit queer, and Elizabeth Carter might be the queerest of the Blues" (Lanser 2003: 275). If any of that nuanced consideration has resonance, then the figure of Minerva as an icon for Elizabeth Carter raises questions that need further consideration. At the least, Minerva's iconographic virtue and chastity keep Carter in a safe zone of reputation, perhaps as a handy strategic cover-up for the intensity of female friendships and an enlarged range of female sexualities.

Angelica Kauffman

The mythological figure of Minerva also raises questions when considering the life, work and reputation of Angelica Kauffman, another iconic eighteenth-century woman of intellect and accomplishment who likewise was featured among the nine "Living Muses of Great Britain." Like Elizabeth Carter, Angelica Kauffman (1741–1807) was a celebrity. Swiss-born, with contacts in circles of artists and writers across Europe, she was trained by her father, a decorative painter who had ecclesiastical and noble clients in many places. Recognized early on as a prodigy, she lived in Italy as a young woman painter, moved to London when she was in her mid-twenties and became established as a painter there from the 1760s into the 1780s. She was active in the art world of eighteenth-century London and was a founding member of the Royal Academy of Arts. Kauffman later was based in Rome for two decades from the 1780s where she ran a studio with her Venetian painter husband and had a salon, with women artists as frequent guests. Kauffman became wealthy and was financially independent. In her long and successful career, she epitomized "painting" for many.

Kauffman was not a court painter but rather an independent artist who worked on commissions from clients. Her main income was from portraiture, including family group portraits of royalty and nobility, and many portraits of women of high social rank. She also was a history painter at a time when narrative history painting was at the top of the hierarchy of genres for artists, and when it was decidedly bold for a woman artist to put herself into this professional and male company (Roworth 2003). Capitalizing on the cachet of classical antiquity in the cultural vocabulary of eighteenth-century Europe, Kauffman worked with many historical, mythological and allegorical themes and stories. Vestal Virgins were one popular theme for artists, for example, and Kauffman did several paintings on this motif that signalled Roman antiquity as well as chastity and self-sacrifice. Kauffman's references to classical Rome were particularly prized in the fine arts and applied arts in England, and her designs were widely reproduced in interior design (wallpaper, on furniture) and household ornament (candy-boxes, and coffee and tea sets); engravings of her work were highly marketable.

Nowadays, when many feminist scholars are interested in issues and

Figure 3 – Angelica Kauffman, Self-portrait with Bust of Minerva" (1780/81)
Oil on canvas, 93 x 76.5 cm,
Bündner Kunstmuseum, Chur, on loan from Gottfried Keller Foundation

practices of identity and self-formation, feminist art historians have given prominence to self-portraits such as those by Angelica Kauffman. Right across her life span, Kauffman painted various prototypes of her own artistic identity and artistic self-creation. Here too she made extensive use of classical and allegorical references. One famous self-portrait, "Angelica Kauffman Hesitating between the Arts of Music and Painting," shows her being tugged between two different muses, that of painting and that of music, both areas of study and skill for Kauffman. Many self-portraits show her holding a sketchbook and pencil or drawing implement.

Nearly half a century after John Fayram's portrait of "Elizabeth Carter as Minerva," this same mythological goddess figures in Kauffman's iconography as well. Minerva's domains included the arts, and Kauffman drew upon this symbolism in her "Self-portrait with Bust of Minerva" (1775–80). Painted when she was in her mid-30s, the portrait shows the artist as a self-assured woman and painter, holding a portfolio and drawing implement (see figure 3). According to art historian Melissa Hyde, women artists of the eighteenth century used the image of Minerva as patron goddess of the arts in their work in order to claim status for themselves. Including Minerva in a female portrait could also identify the sitter as a patron of the arts, and add an element of seriousness to the representation. This versatile goddess was part of what Kauffman scholar Angela Rosenthal has termed Kauffman's "visual rhetoric of the female intellectual portrait" (Rosenthal 2006: 168).

Minerva was a good choice of icon for Angelica Kauffman, for Kauffman clearly worked very hard on her self-image in her art and life. She sought a particular public image and many of her self-portraits figure her as dedicated, firm, forthright, direct and professional — not alluring or unbridled. She took the path of self-command and discretion in her self-fashioning as a woman artist working professionally and with very few female counterparts who were taken seriously. As both an artist and a woman of society, she also had to keep decorum and be a professional exemplar. It is notable that she clothed herself in her "Self-Portrait with Bust of Minerva" in garments that are evidence of status and standing. Her brightly colored robes, trimmed with fur, place her in high company. She is a mainstream celebrity, well-armoured, socially secure, established and civilized.

Looking across the large number of female figures in Angelica Kauffman's paintings, it is striking, in this regard, how few examples there are in her work of female nudes or even partially unclothed women. One painting that stands out because it is unusual within her *oeuvre* dates from 1790 and portrays Flora, the Roman goddess of flowers (see figure 4). This painting of the goddess of flowers, draped but with bare breasts and belly, was done by Kauffman as a special request by the man who commissioned it; the painting is still in a private collection (Baumgärtel 1998: 257). An unclothed and alluring Flora was not part of Angelica Kauffman's public image as an artist, either in representation or in self-representation, and found no place in her own repertoire of self-fashioning. This was a wise choice for Kauffman because Flora was a problematic icon for women in the later eighteenth century who cultivated their place in culture and society.

Figure 4 – Angelica Kauffman, "Flora" (1790) Oil on canvas, 68.5 x 51 cm Private collection, Vorarlberg

Flora

Mythologies throughout the world have some version of a Flora figure, an aspect of nature associated with springtime and renewal. At times Flora represents rural innocence and simplicity in idyllic pastoral contexts. More often, Flora's realm is the material domain of nature that has to do with plants and flowers and with reproduction. She is anchored in the body, sexed female and gendered feminine. In Roman mythology, Flora is one of the terrestrial goddesses, and over the centuries, during the Renaissance and coming into early modern Europe, she was depicted in many guises. One is as the nurturing mother of flowers who generates growth through her body's milk, and is conventionally shown with full breasts and a rounded belly. Another is Flora as the Queen of Flowers, a figure of power who presides, along with Pomona, goddess of flowers, and Ceres, goddess of grain, over seasonal and agricultural cycles of rebirth and fruition. Across the long eighteenth century, spectators and readers would have been familiar with these figures of Flora. She was in garden statuary based on models from classical antiquity. She was portrayed in historical and mythological paintings. She was invoked in poetry and visualized in book frontispieces (Shteir 2006).

Since discourses of sexuality and female bodies are central features of any Flora storyline, accounts of the goddess of flowers are never simple and always culturally fraught. She has been gendered and embodied in ways that sometimes represent power, pleasure, agency and knowledge, but often convey versions of womankind that are meant to be derogatory (Shteir 2006). Mythology textbooks for young people and for use in schools that were in circulation across the entire eighteenth century tell a story about Flora that has nothing to do with mothers or queens or springtime. They present her instead as a prostitute associated with nakedness and fraudulance. We can witness this in *Tooke's Pantheon*, a collection of stories about gods and goddesses that was the mythographic best seller of the long eighteenth century. Flora appears there as part of the Floralia, an event in the Roman religious year when ritualized theatrical events were staged in honor of the goddess as a way to ensure her favor. These included burlesque performances by prostitutes, who took off their clothes on audience demand (Shteir 2007). Tooke introduces Flora in his mythology textbook as "the Goddess and President of Flowers" (Tooke 1976: 249), but then goes on to unmask her. The goddess Flora, he declares, was herself really a prostitute, and the lewdness of her performance shows the shame of heathen Rome. There are a number of back-stories at work here, with various ways to unpack this image of Flora, having to do with the poet Ovid, Roman politics, Christian apologetics and gender-differentiated models of conduct and value. *Tooke's Pantheon* was written in Latin in 1659, translated into English in 1698, revised and reprinted more than twenty-five times across the 1700s and widely adapted for use in schools for elite males in eighteenth-century England, a time that aspired to Roman practices and values. It can be read, therefore, as having both a religious function and a social function, especially as a pedagogy that reproduces the social relations of Augustan Rome for Augustan England. It is telling in this regard that Tooke's account of Flora is a censorious representation of women, gendered reputation and dishonor. His depiction of the goddess of flowers as a prostitute was mirrored in numerous other mythology textbooks that were circulating when Angelica Kauffman did her commissioned portrait of a naked Flora in 1790.

In comparison with the 1770s, when Angelica Kauffman represented herself as Minerva and when Bluestocking gatherings were in full swing, it became considerably harder by the 1790s to be an intellectual woman. Yet this was the very time when science was being promoted as part of general culture and when interest in the workings of nature was being cultivated for new audiences. Botany — the scientific study of plants — began to take shape as an area separate from medicine, and was one area of particularly heightened intellectual involvement by women, who cultivated their own botanical interests and were cultivated in turn by educators and others with Enlightenment intentions (Shteir 1996). Women's education continued to be encouraged as a social good, but fears of Bluestocking feminism were coupled with conservative reaction in England to political and social turmoil in revolutionary France. One result was what historian Dror Wahrman has

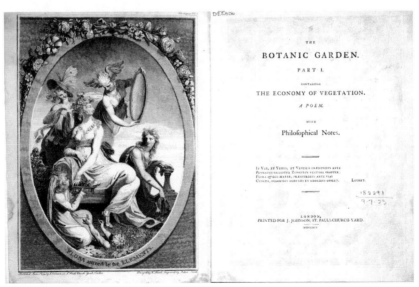

Figure 5 – Henry Fuseli, "Flora attir'd by the Elements," frontispiece to Erasmus Darwin, *The Botanic Garden* (1789–91).
The Thomas Fisher Rare Book Library, University of Toronto.

termed "gender panic" in the late eighteenth century, when fears about blurring differences between women and men led to backlash about parameters and types of practice for women (Wahrman 2004). In these contexts, representations of the goddess Flora are one way to gauge shifts and tensions in the cultural climate of those decades.

Some contradictions between late Enlightenment ideas and gender agendas are visible in a poem by Erasmus Darwin (grandfather of Charles Darwin). Darwin was a progressive thinker who wanted to popularize new botanical ideas so that more people — notably, more women — could have access to knowledge of nature and science. He wrote *The Botanic Garden* (1789–91), a scientific work in verse, as a way to promote "polite" science for women. The artist Henry Fuseli was commissioned to do the frontispiece, entitled "Flora attir'd by the Elements," which dates from the same time as Kauffman's commissioned Flora (see figure 5). Fuseli portrayed Flora as a force of nature being dressed by symbolic figures of Earth, Air, Fire and Water for her work as a goddess in the plant kingdom. She is represented as an attractive and enticing fashionable young woman sitting in a sinuous pose. The juxtaposition of images of Flora, Elizabeth Carter and Angelica Kauffman is striking. John Fayram puts Elizabeth Carter in the company of Minerva and Plato, and Angelica Kauffman portrays herself holding the tools of a working artist. By contrast, Fuseli's Flora is preoccupied with her mirror, depicted as an instrument not for truth-seeking so much as for ornament, self-involvement and self-display.

By the 1790s, when Fuseli's Flora was part of polite culture, Minerva had lost hold as a female icon. As Mary Wollstonecraft herself learned all too well, a female intellectual swam in perilous waters at that time. During the decades from the 1790s across the 1830s, a new kind of essentialized feminized ideal was promoted for women, having to do with feeling rather than mind and domesticity rather than intellectuality. In light of what I have been discussing, it was almost predictable that a British women's magazine in 1817 would warn women away from botany and other sciences. Thus, a correspondent wrote in as a member of a "Green-Stocking Club," which was formed, she explains, by women who opposed bluestocking intellectual activities and aims. "Absolute chaos" would result from any blurring of male and female domains, so she exhorts women to be not blue but "green," to know their place and to be in the kitchen rather than the botanical garden (Shteir 2004: 3).

Concluding Points

What can feminist cultural history learn from the eighteenth-century female celebrities and icons I have been discussing? How can the Bluestockings, Elizabeth Carter, Angelica Kauffman and Minerva and Flora help us reconsider feminist knowledge? I offer some reflections as instigation to practice.

First, feminist cultural history should be written with large and bold strokes, recapturing some of the sense of indignation that characterized publications from chapters of feminist thought going back several centuries. Judith M. Bennett, for example, in *History Matters: Patriarchy and the Challenge of Feminism* (2006), has recuperated patriarchy as a category for historical scholarship and as a tool for tracking continuities and mechanisms across centuries. Always, though, as Bennett's own work on medieval and early-modern women demonstrates, analyses have a sharper edge when they are historicized and anchored in local practices and immediate contexts. It is in the local versions and applications of patriarchy that we can identify and unpack the workings of ideas about gendered hierarchies, power and authority. In this regard, I would like feminist researchers and Women's Studies teachers, students, and scholars to take the past more seriously, to be less presentist in orientation and to integrate historical material and approaches more routinely into practices of teaching and learning. This is equally important in undergraduate introductory classes and graduate research seminars.

Second, feminist engagement with the past has been greatly enhanced by resources that now are available. Online sources and digitized materials offer fresh and local access to earlier primary materials and provide unprecedented access to materials for studying women in relation to culture and history in ways that complicate stories and should guide scholars away from monolithic accounts. Many authors who were widely known and read in the eighteenth century but then disappeared are being recuperated and made available to new generations of readers. Within histories of women's cultural production, new emphases on writing rather than on literature highlight work by women in genres that became less canonical, including historical and pedagogical writing, translation, and writing for magazines. The recent print publication *Rational Passions: Women and Scholarship in Britain, 1702–1870* anthologizes selections of women's intellectual work, including selections from writings by Elizabeth Carter and several other Bluestockings (Gordon and Walker 2008). A major exhibit about the historical Bluestockings of eighteenth-century England was on display at the National Portrait Gallery in London in 2008, and the catalogue has been published under the title *Brilliant Women* (Eger and Peltz 2008). Along with thousands of letters written by Bluestockings to one another, collected volumes of their writings now make Bluestocking energy available for us to tap into in ways that have not been recoverable for more than two centuries, and scholars have been busy reconsidering them as a historically specific group of intellectual women (Kelly 1999; Pohl and Schellenberg 2003). Similarly, within histories of women's art, work is being rediscovered, brought (like the portrait of Elizabeth Carter as Minerva) from private collections into public display or once again made available (like the portrait of the "Nine Living Muses") for cultural diagnosis. The centrality of the visual as a resource for us in the early twenty-first century can jumpstart attention to the power of art, media and popular culture in earlier times. Portraits and self-portraits of Angelica Kauffman supply many windows onto the worlds in which she lived and worked, and I doubt that they were much different from what Amelia Jones in *The Feminism and Visual Culture Reader* has termed "the image culture in which we are suspended" (Jones 2003: 3).

The history of science is yet another resource for fresh consideration about women in relation to culture and history. Women pursued knowledge of nature in many geographical sites and through multiple practices. Taking science as part of culture, an abundance of textual, visual, and material evidence then emerges for women's work within eighteenth-century sciences as collectors, educators, journalists, textbook writers, teachers, experimenters, artists, collaborators, correspondents, poets and translators, mediating knowledge and creating it anew. The picture of early science changes when the parameters enlarge.

Next, new textual, visual and material resources and new ways of reading can bring us closer to the tensions and complexities for actual women in earlier times. More texts and expanded repertoires of approaches will show that we are not the first generation of women to juggle and self-fashion. In the past as in the present, many different voices are at play in any time or any place. Some are dominant and shape tone and atmosphere, encouraging access or channeling it. Other voices are less dominant but no less present. The layeredness of eighteenth-century England is, I suggest, the layeredness of modern feminisms, and there are many feminist cultural histories still to be written across the dynamic spectrum of humankind.

It is highly likely that in most times and places we can find examples of how an individual woman or group of women struggled at intersections, negotiated, positioned herself, resisted, failed to thrive, pushed at boundaries, subverted and critiqued.

Feminist cultural history will be enriched by looking, looking more and looking again at groups and individuals in the past. Seek for how they are like us, or pursue their fundamental otherness. Learn to follow your own feminist nose. Be feminist scholar-adventurers: climb the fence to find information in an overgrown cemetery. Look beyond biographies or autobiographies that feel expurgated and do not match how you encounter life. After Elizabeth Carter's death in 1806, her nephew compiled a memoir and volumes of her correspondence by cutting and pasting, excluding what did not fulfill his notion of her piety and virtue. This became a Life and Letters portrait of Elizabeth Carter that spoke to his icon but not to Carter as her own person with her own experiences and realities. At the same time we must hold carefully in mind that these experiences and realities are mediated by socioeconomic circumstances and other intersectionalities, and also mediated by cultural symbols, belief structures and power relations that set the tone and atmosphere and that form a cultural imaginary.

Mythology and iconographies come in here as stories and associations passed along through time and space as part of cultural traditions, and often with remarkable staying power. Myths about the goddess Flora, for example, represented ideas and values and also conveyed and confirmed them. No differently from now, as poststructuralist work has helped us understand, myths are not monolithic narrative building blocks. Versions change, emphases shift. Artists and writers in the eighteenth century had vocabulary for using mythology, and they chose to use it in their work. Most of us do not have that degree of knowledge of the symbolic repertoire of myths and their meanings. Yet it would enhance our feminist tool chests if we did. For the Romans of classical antiquity, gods and goddesses had some kinds of reality within religious beliefs and/or ritual practices. So it was too for the Greeks and across cultural traditions more generally. Goddesses like Minerva and Flora hover just outside peripheral vision, as forces whose powers needed to be acknowledged, addressed, honored and propitiated. These goddesses are cultural ghosts, figures in an ongoing cultural imaginary. We would be wrong to ignore them, for their powers persist and compel our attention. Give restitution to Minerva, therefore, or else! Find Flora behind those patriarchal panels, or else! Give fresh cultural authority to Elizabeth Carter and the Bluestockings, or else! We should recover lost knowledges and thereby help them to live again. Otherwise there is every possibility that we too will disappear from the record of history, perhaps to be rediscovered by later generations and waves of feminist history.

Alternately, we can pay attention as teachers, students, activists and scholars, and make room for the Bluestockings, Elizabeth Carter and Angelica Kauffman, and for Minerva and Flora in the women's studies classroom and other feminist forums. Many scholars have done the work upon which we build in the present moment. Recent cadres of feminists, at York University and elsewhere, have had the privilege of affiliation with lively and creative bluestocking circles of intellectual women. Mindful of complexities, and valiantly aiming to be intersectional, feminist academics value sociability and the power of talk. We set ourselves heavy tasks in the classroom and in our institutional responsibilities, and also in our individual research projects. But we are not the first or second generation of feminist scholars that is seeking to shape knowledge that will change the world. Scholarship is feminist activism too, and we should be making it work for us.

References

Banier, Abbé Antoine. 1976. *Mythology and Fables of the Ancients Explain'd from History* 1738. (Trans. London, 1739-40.) New York: Garland.

Baskins, Cristelle, and Lisa Rosenthal (eds.). 2007. *Early Modern Visual Allegory: Embodying Meaning*. Aldershot, Hamps: Ashgate.

Baumgärtel, Bettina. 1998. *Angelika Kauffman*. Düsseldorf: Verlag Gerd Hatje.

Bennett, Judith M. 2006. *History Matters: Patriarchy and the Challenge of Feminism*. Philadelphia: University of Pennsylvania Press.

Blathwayt, Janice E. 2002. "More than Distinguished for 'Piety and Virtue': New Perspectives on Elizabeth Carter." Ph.D. thesis, York University.

Bluestocking Bookstore. n.d. "Our Mission." <bluestockings.com>.

Carter, Elizabeth. 1989. "A Dialogue." In *Eighteenth-Century Women Poets: An Oxford Anthology*. (Ed. Roger Lonsdale.) Oxford: Oxford University Press.

Crow, Barbara A. (ed.). 2000. *Radical Feminism: A Documentary Reader*. New York: New York University Press.

Darwin, Erasmus. 1973. *The Botanic Garden* (1789–91). Menston, Yorkshire: Scolar Press.

Doherty, Lillian E. 2001. *Gender and the Interpretation of Classical Myth*. London: Duckworth.

Eger, Elizabeth. 2010. *Bluestockings: Women of Reason from Enlightenment to Romanticism*. New York: Palgrave Macmillan.

Eger, Elizabeth, and Lucy Peltz. 2008. *Brilliant Women: Eighteenth-Century Bluestockings*. London: National Portrait Gallery.

Feldman, Burton, and Robert D. Richardson, Jr. 1972. *The Rise of Modern Mythology 1680–1860*. Bloomington: Indiana University Press.

Gordon, Felicia, and Gina Luria Walker (eds.). 2008. *Rational Passions: Women and Scholarship in Britain, 1702–1870*. Peterborough, ON: Broadview Press.

Hyde, Melissa. 2003. "Under the Sign of Minerva: Adélaïde Labille-Guiard's *Portrait of Madame Adélaïde*," *Women, Art and the Politics of Identity in Eighteenth-Century Europe*. (Ed. Melissa Hyde and Jennifer Milam.) Aldershot: Ashgate.

Jones, Amelia. 2003. *The Feminism and Visual Culture Reader*. London: Routledge.

Kelly, Gary (ed.). 1999. *Bluestocking Feminism: Writings of the Bluestocking Circle, 1738–1785*. (6 vols.) London: Pickering & Chatto.

Knott, Sarah, and Barbara Taylor (eds.). 2005. *Women, Gender and Enlightenment*. Basingstoke, Hamps: Palgrave Macmillan.

Lanser, Susan. 2003. "Bluestocking Sapphism and the Economies of Desire." In Nicole Pohl and Betty A. Schellenberg (eds.), *Reconsidering the Bluestockings*. San Marino, CA: Huntington Library.

Le Doeuff, Michèle. 2003. *The Sex of Knowing*. (Trans. Kathryn Hamer and Lorraine Code.) London: Routledge.

Peltz, Lucy. 2008. "Living Muses: Constructing and Celebrating the Professional Woman in Literature and the Arts." In Elizabeth Eger and Lucy Peltz (eds.), *Brilliant Women: Eighteenth-Century Bluestockings*. London: National Portrait Gallery.

Pohl, Nicole, and Betty A. Schellenberg (eds.). 2003. *Reconsidering the Bluestockings*. San Marino, CA: Huntington Library.

Rosenthal, Angela. 2006. *Angelica Kauffman: Art and Sensibility*. New Haven and London:

Yale University Press.

Roworth, Wendy Wassyng. 2003. "Ancient Matrons and Modern Patrons: Angelica Kauffman as a Classical History Painter." In Melissa Hyde and Jennifer Milam (eds.), *Women, Art and the Politics of Identity in Eighteenth-Century Europe*. Aldershot: Ashgate.

Shteir, Ann B. 2007. "*Flora primavera* or *Flora meretrix*? Iconography, Gender, and Science." *Studies in Eighteenth-Century Culture* 36. Baltimore: Johns Hopkins University Press.

___. 2006. "Iconographies of Flora." In Ann B. Shteir and Bernard Lightman (eds.), *Figuring It Out: Science, Gender, and Visual Culture*. Hanover, NH: Dartmouth College Press.

___. 2004. "Green-Stocking or Blue? Science in Three Women's Magazines, 1800–50." In Louise Henson et al. (eds.), *Culture and Science in the Nineteenth-Century Media*. Aldershot: Ashgate.

___. 1996. *Cultivating Women, Cultivating Science: Flora's Daughters and Botany in England, 1760 to 1860*. Baltimore: Johns Hopkins University Press.

Tooke, Andrew. 1976. *The Pantheon, Representing the Fabulous Histories of the Heathen Gods and Most Illustrious Heroes in a Short, Plain and Familiar Method* [1713]. (Ed. 6.) New York: Garland.

Wahrman, Dror. 2004. *The Making of the Modern Self: Identity and Culture in Eighteenth-Century England*. New Haven: Yale University Press.

Woolf, Virginia. 1975 [1928]. *A Room of One's Own*. Harmondsworth, Middlesex: Penguin Books.

Chapter Seven

FEMINISM, ECOLOGICAL THINKING AND THE LEGACY OF RACHEL CARSON

Lorraine Code

Rachel Carson and Ecological Thinking

In *Ecological Thinking: The Politics of Epistemic Location* (Code 2006) I turn to
Rachel Carson, to read between the lines of her texts — especially *Silent
Spring* (Carson 1962) — en route to developing an epistemological approach
I call *ecological naturalism*. I begin by recalling how the dominant theories of
knowledge of post-Industrial-Revolution, affluent, western-northern societies
have been complicit in producing and perpetuating a rhetoric of mastery
and possession. Central to that rhetoric is an imagery of knowledge acquired
for purposes of manipulating, predicting and controlling nature and human
nature, animated by representations of knowledge as a prized commodity
which is capable of legitimating its possessors' authoritative occupancy (and
sometime abuse) of positions of power, as they recast the natural world as a
resource for human gratification. The late-twentieth-century ecology movement's critical stance vis-à-vis an energy-fetishised society's unquestioning
reliance on a simplistic, unreconstructed scientistic methodology for acquir-
ing knowledge of nature and human nature is now well known. In the early
twenty-first century, critiques of scientism have become a central focus of
revisionary social-political inquiry, praxis and contestation, both feminist and
other, beyond anything Carson could have imagined.[1]

Rachel Carson (1907–1964) was an eminent American marine biologist
and nature writer who is credited with having founded the modern environmental movement. After abandoning her doctoral studies for financial
reasons, Carson embarked on a career as a biologist with the U.S. Bureau of
Fisheries, moving on to become a full-time nature writer in the 1950s. From
her early sea trilogy, *Under the Sea Wind* (1941), *The Sea Around Us* (1950) and *The
Edge of the Sea* (1955), she gained enduring acclaim as a gifted nature writer.
Yet because she came to be deeply disturbed by the increasingly profligate
use of chemical pesticides, especially after World War II, Carson shifted
her focus to concentrate on studying, documenting and warning politicians
and the public about the long-term effects of pesticides, and in particular of
DDT. In *Silent Spring*, which brought environmental issues to the attention of

unprecedented numbers of Americans, she challenges the pesticide spraying practices of agricultural scientists and the policies of the U.S. government that supported them, and calls for radically reconceiving the relationships between human beings and the natural world. *Silent Spring* prompted a reversal in national pesticide policy, leading to a nationwide ban on DDT and several other pesticides. The book and the grassroots environmental movement it inspired led to the founding of the U.S. Environmental Protection Agency. Carson was posthumously awarded the Presidential Medal of Freedom by former U.S. President Jimmy Carter. Yet, in her time, and still today, Carson has been attacked as an alarmist and even as a "murderer" by the chemical industry and by other policy makers and climate-change deniers (see Oreskes and Conway 2010).

Social and political commitments permeate Rachel Carson's own scientific practice, if often implicitly, in research that was indisputably ecological well before that term achieved common currency in everyday English and in professional scientific circles. As it has evolved — albeit unevenly and contentiously — to inform late-twentieth- and early-twenty-first-century ecological science and environmental activism, Carson's legacy is impressive for its potential to unsettle the settled assumptions of an epistemological orthodoxy that sustains a conviction in the epistemic and political value of individual, depersonalized mastery and control. By contrast, a commitment to collaborative democratic conversation and negotiation characterizes her manner of weaving scientific and extra-scientific evidence together, and of circulating her findings to an often sceptical public. Her work, in effect, entered the public arena with the power to interrupt the complacency and hubris of "man's" presumptive dominion over all the earth. To people who know Carson as a path-breaking practitioner of ecological thinking and action, these claims will not be new. But it is important to recall that it is possible, both then and now, to work as a naturalist, even as an environmentalist or a wildlife scientist, without thinking ecologically. What, then, makes Carson's work distinctively ecological? And why do I commend it to epistemologists and to feminists, on these grounds?

According to her biographer, Linda Lear, it was when she was gathering material in the early 1950s for *The Edge of the Sea* that Carson's thinking shifted from being primarily geographical to being explicitly ecological. It shifted toward becoming a process of producing a "biographical sketch" in order to explain the "special features of each environment to which creatures… [had] to adapt"; to studying their "life cycles and physical habitats" and identifying the "ways in which they had adapted to various and often continuously changing conditions" (Lear 1977: 229). From this reconfigured position, Carson began to study different types of shore — rock, sand and coral — writing about "each geological area as a living ecological community

rather than about individual organisms" (243). As her commitment to ecological thinking developed and consolidated, Carson turned to characterize
the scope of biology as "the history of the earth and all its life — the past,
the present, and the future," adding, "neither man [sic] nor any other living
creature may be studied or comprehended apart from the world in which
he lives" (Carson quoted in Lear 1977: 278). In this claim, which would become pivotal to her ongoing work, she echoes a point from her acceptance
speech for the National Book Award where she insists: "It is impossible to
understand man without understanding his environment and the forces
that have molded him physically and environmentally" (Carson quoted in
Lear 1977: 219). Additionally, without understanding how "he," in turn, has
made and is constantly unmaking and remaking that environment. Such is
her ecological credo.

Carson's point must be read with great care if its epistemological potential is to be realized. She is not proposing that environmental "forces"
determine who and what "man" is or can be, nor that they determine the
processes and products of knowledge making. Her (often-implicit) contention
throughout her research is that the constitutive effects of environmental forces,
broadly conceived, need to be sought out, taken carefully into account, and
evaluated *in situ*. But to insist that they are crucially influential does not imply
that these effects are automatic in a quasi-mechanistic sense; or that they are
identical from place to place, phenomenon to phenomenon. Translated into
the realm of knowledge-seeking processes, then, the implication is that where,
when, how and by whom knowledge is made and circulated often needs to
be investigated in evaluating the knowledge itself: that it is implausible and
indeed careless to assume without question that knowledge transcends the
circumstances of its making, to claim universal pertinence. In light of these
considerations, I am proposing that there are points of continuity between
Carson's ecological thinking and Donna Haraway's work on "situated knowledges" (Haraway 1991), which I read as showing how "situation" becomes a
place to know: both a place where epistemic activity occurs; and a place that
demands to be known in its aspects that facilitate or thwart knowing well. Such
an analysis would map the structural intricacies of place, the materialities,
demographies, genealogies, commitments and power relations that shape
the knowledge and subjectivities enacted there; the intractable locational
specificities that resist homogenization; the positionings available or closed
to would-be knowers. Situation, on such a reading, is not just a place from
which to know, as the language of "perspectives" implies, indifferently available to anyone who chooses to stand there: it is an achieved stance, integral
to "the politics of epistemic location."

In *Ecological Thinking* I enlist Carson's ideas to shape a working epistemology and I elaborate them metaphorically to explain through extended

examples (one of which I will outline here) why knowing ecologically claims greater potential than dislocated knowledge projects, to do epistemic justice to subject matters, circumstances, actions and events. A focus on habitat as a place to know is central to my argument. Extrapolating beyond Carson's own writings, I propose that social, political, cultural and experiential elements figure alongside physical and (other) environmental contributors to the nature of a habitat and its inhabitants at any historical moment, and are therefore integral to conditions for the production of knowledge there. Thus, from pieces of her writings and the stories her biographers and commentators tell, I have assembled a picture of Carson as epistemologist, whose practices of inquiry, "style(s) of reasoning," and rhetorical strategies contrast with those of a (perhaps caricatured) post-positivist faith in the power of a dislocated, monolithic, spectator science to explain everything worthy of explanation. This contrast has to be developed with care, however, for the strength of Carson's position in *Silent Spring* as in her earlier books resides in her informed, judicious respect for empirical, observational evidence: her scientific credentials are firmly in place. Carson is no naive anti-science crusader, as feminist and other critics of "big science" are often charged with being. Indeed, Carson is best characterized as an objective realist, both in the value she accords to knowing the natural world carefully and well in the minutiae of its detail and their interconnections, and on knowing the implications of treating, living in, relating to the world in certain ways. Yet the version of empiricism that runs through her work departs from classical empiricism in virtue of her refusal to treat the world as a machine, comprised of discrete, comprehensible, controllable bits. It departs further in its emphasis on understanding and wisdom, and in its explicit, if contentious, infusion with values, which are as ethical as they are ecological and conservational; and it departs from that mechanistic tradition in her commitment to knowing well enough to respond respectfully to the world in the specificity of its detail (see Cafaro 2008). In her view, proof was not confined to the laboratory, nor were scientific and ethical issues separable from one another: a distinction between spectator and participant knowledge gathering catches some of the substance of this contrast. In this regard, her work invites a reading through principles of epistemic responsibility (see Code 1987).

All of this notwithstanding, Carson was, and has continued to be, as vilified as she was acclaimed (especially for *Silent Spring*), even though her research practice was scientifically exacting and responsible by most of the criteria of mid-twentieth-century science. As one commentator puts it, in cutting "against the grain of materialism, scientism, and the technologically engineered control of nature" her work subverts some of the most basic assumptions of instituted scientific practice (Kroll 2002: 20). It generates a healthy skepticism about reductive, mechanistic research that isolates parts of nature so as to obscure the constitutive functions — the enabling and/or constraining influences — of multiple, complex interconnections in producing and sustaining the phenomena it studies. Yet Carson's at-first-blush curious reputation as a subversive thinker and practitioner animates my reading of her methodology. I celebrate her subversiveness with respect to questions of evidence, to the circulation of knowledge and to the challenge she offers to scientific hubris: hence I commend Mark Hamilton Lytle for having entitled his impressive book *The Gentle Subversive: Rachel Carson, Silent Spring, and the Rise of the Environmental Movement* (Lytle 2007). But the question is, why was she seen, more generally, as subversive? It is an interesting question to which I will explore some (interim) answers.

Part of the explanation bears upon the rhetorical, conceptual architecture of the scientific and epistemological world — upon the epistemic and scientific imaginary — that infused the professional domain where Carson's research and activism took place, which was structured by stark hierarchical evaluative divisions. Those that pertain to this analysis are the divisions between fact and anecdote, truth and narrative, reason and feeling, of which the first item in each pair has consistently claimed greater public and professional credibility, authority and reliability than the second. The division is governed by an objective/subjective dichotomy that locates anecdote, narrative and feeling on the negative, subjective side, contending that it is in facts alone, dispassionately acquired, that truth is to be found. Especially in her respect for testimonial evidence, by which I mean people's reports of their everyday, down-on-the-ground experiences, which are often relegated to the merely anecdotal, Carson's epistemic practice unsettles such stark distinctions and earns the label "subversive," in part, from so doing. These distinctions originate in the Anglo-American empiricist tradition where perception, memory and testimony count as the principal sources of knowledge and are ranked in that order, with perception counting as the most basic and reliable of the three, memory ranking second best and testimony regarded as a distant third. The rhetoric that holds this distinction in place conflates testimony with hearsay, rumour, mere opinion, gossip, thus contrasting it with the presumptively more direct, secure, reliable perception and memory and establishing grounds for dismissing it as merely anecdotal. In her research practice Carson defied this ranking and was criticized for so doing. Yet her capacity to bring together scientific and experiential evidence is one of her more remarkable achievements, as she works across diverse modes of knowledge, domains of inquiry and subject matters to produce conclusions that are sufficiently specific to address the distinctiveness of precisely individuated local phenomena; sufficiently cognizant of wider patterns in nature to generate hypotheses for knowing other, analogous phenomena; sufficiently informed and coherent to engage with the agendas of policy-makers, the doubts of disbelievers and the bewilderment of a lay public caught between so-called expert scientific assurances and experiential incongruities. Carson shows by example how the very complexity of each separate subject matter she deals with requires her, as knower, to be multilingual and multiply literate: to speak the language of laboratory science, wildlife organizations, government agencies, chemical-producing companies, secular nature lovers and many others; to understand the detail of scientific documents and the force of everyday experience; to work back and forth between variations on the imagery of mastery and ecology — sometimes, all for the sake of understanding something so very small as a beetle.

More specifically and perhaps curiously, the methodological and politics-of-knowledge issues that fuel suspicions of testimony as a source of evidence still today — hence the widespread disdain in her time for Carson's reliance on it — derive from the (lowly) status of experience in positivist-empiricist knowledge projects. Such projects accord minimal authority to individual, concrete, first-person reports of people's experiences, contrasted with a controlled, formal experience that is everyone's and no one's. Feminist and other postcolonial theorists of knowledge, aware of the hierarchies of power and privilege whose effects are to valorize some people's experiential claims — their testimony — and denigrate others', are familiar with vexed and vexatious questions about how experience can stand as evidence and about whose experiences count and why, given how unevenly credibility is distributed across the social order and how often testimony is discounted because of whose it is. Understandably, in view of the apolitical epistemic climate of her time, Carson is less interested in the identity or social-political positioning of a testifier than in the substance of the testimony. But this issue is alive and urgent in current feminist, anti-racist and other postcolonial theories of knowledge and ignorance, and Carson herself knew how it was to be mocked and discredited for her reliance on word-of-mouth evidence.

With these thoughts in mind, I turn to an example from a different domain, in order to show, metaphorically, how knowing ecologically can contribute to promoting epistemic justice in knowing people, subject matters, circumstances, actions and events. This example displays a version of ecological thinking at work in its manner of revalorizing experiential evidence by engaging in practices of inquiry that move away from entrenched patterns of dismissing and discrediting it. I draw on structural similarities between Carson's ecological approach and Canadian biologist Karen Messing's feminist-informed research on women's occupational health: research that I read as similarly ecological, on an analogy with Carson's knowledge-gathering practices. As Carson maps the local and wider effects of pesticides, so Messing and her colleagues rely on scientific-observational and experiential evidence culled from interview upon interview with workers, union members and other "ordinary folk" in specific workplace settings, to investigate how "women workers and scientists can be brought together to make occupational health studies more accurate and effective in improving working conditions" (Messing 1978: xvi). When symptoms are specific to very small groups of workers, analysts commonly fail to recognize their significance, contending that they afford insufficient (statistical) certainty either to establish the reality of suffering, or to substantiate workers' compensation claims. Having observed such failures, Messing was prompted to investigate how minutely individuated complaints play themselves out for specific people (usually, in her studies, women) in the particularities of workplaces, habitats and environments governed by an ethos of profit and efficiency and backed by an epistemology reliant on statistical certainty. Her practice, like Carson's, is as subversive as it is respectful of the norms of scientific inquiry, notably in the place she accords to specific, situated testimony in the production of knowledge. Messing reads statistical evidence against the resistance of certain problems and symptoms to inclusion under law-like descriptions, moving between the laboratory and the workplace floor much as Carson moves between the laboratory and the field or the ocean floor. Her work, too, is marked by an interplay between local hypotheses and empirical generalizations, where analogies from one set of problems or symptoms to another may move inquiry forward, disanalogies may initiate productive rethinking.

Frustrated by repeated attempts to convince unions, employers, and workers themselves of the factuality of correlations between specific workplace conditions and women's health, Messing (1978: 19) sees a vicious circle in which "researchers do not think of looking for an occupational cause… such causes are not demonstrated, so the problems are attributed to women's biological or psychological 'nature'." Her aim is to undermine the injustices such stereotype-reliant "naturalizing" (25) enacts, together with the unspoken assumption it engenders to the effect that if something can be labelled "natural" then it counts as given, immutable: it is pointless to try to change it. Arguing that such assumptions contribute to the very naturalizing such appeals to nature perform, Messing demonstrates that women's workplace health has less to do with generic female incapacities, more to do with standards of fitness based on fixed ideas about jobs, equipment, work environments and attitudes drawn from what is imagined to be typical for men. She maintains, "even when a biological characteristic has an important genetic component, it can be changed by altering the environment" (26). Thus she shows how work stations, tools and equipment designed for the average man place many women and some men at a disadvantage, whose effects in pain, stress and discomfort are rarely acknowledged except in the language of failing to meet an abstract, one-size-fits-all criterion of fitness. For example, women blue-collar workers report "too-large boots and gloves, too-big shovels, and clippers with too-wide intervals between the handles" (35).

Statistics which show the occupational fatality rate for men to be twelve times the rate for women are commonly read to show that women's jobs are safer than men's, thereby supporting a paternalistic — and tacitly naturalistic — assurance that "job segregation has kept women out of dangerous jobs... protected their health" (13). Messing's research subverts such readings, bringing numerous, often quite bizarre, examples to support her conclusions: women eliminated from a Canadian study of exposure to agricultural chemicals because, in most provincial records, "only the husband of the [presumptively heterosexual] farm family was identified as a farmer" (58); or a doctor informing the International Ergonomics Association that "it had been scientifically proved that *all* carpal tunnel symptoms among older women were due to the menopause" (97).

The politics are complex. When workers turn to activism in an effort to improve their circumstances they may meet with a suspicion that "they will fake symptoms to gain their point" even, Messing notes, when the patterns of physiological change they report are so specific to the toxic effect that a worker "would have to be a specialist... to produce them." (69) A mail sorter who reported extreme arm, shoulder and elbow pain lost a compensation claim because an expert witness "quoted from scientific literature purporting to show that repeated movements could not produce injury below a specific weight manipulated... [and] described his own laboratory tests, which... showed that this type of work was not dangerous" (xv). No one examined the material detail of the sorter's situation (xvi); yet without the knowledge only so location-specific an investigation could provide, these reports claim dubious validity. Hence Messing asks: "*how do scientists decide whom and what to study in the occupational health field?*" (xv, emphasis in original): a pivotal question for feminist and other post-positivist science and epistemology. Adequate answers, I suggest, require attending to the workers' testimony with an initial presumption in favour of their believability, however negotiable their claims may turn out to be; analyzing the detail of their interactions and diverse situatedness ecologically, from a research stance informed and vigilant to detect local, often minuscule, epistemic injustices — testimonial injustices — generated by the politics of knowledge (gendered, raced, classed, aged, ableist and other) and the profit-driven interests that produce patterns of invisibility and insignificance, credulity and incredulity across populations and occupations.

Although Carson and Messing take first-person testimonial reports of environmental and health-specific harms very seriously, theirs is in no respect a naïve experientialism for which reports of experience claim an unchallengeable status. Thus they participate, if inadvertently, in a controversy with which feminists have struggled at least since the early 1970s. Testimony, in their professional inquiry, functions both as evidence and as a catalyst for ongoing investigation: they acknowledge its contestability and its openness to interpretation, while affirming its value. But what, one might ask, could be the problem about experience? The question is central to feminist and other postcolonial work on knowledge and its connections with authority and power. Why can experiential reports so readily be denigrated, dismissed as merely anecdotal? A short answer, within a knowledge economy that holds a residual positivism in place, is that even under the elevated label "testimony," experiential evidence conveyed in first-person tellings is thought inevitably to compromise objectivity and thus to weaken the public credibility of research in which experiential reports are included as part of the evidence. Historically, incredulity in the face of testimony is neither unusual nor surprising, in view of a long lineage of distrust in the putative chaos and unsubstantiated muddle of everyday experience. Nor is it surprising in light of the complex patterns of corroboration that have been required — if inconsistently throughout Western history — to elevate testimony to the status of a (perhaps negotiated) credibility. But the problem, as feminists and other "Others" have amply shown, is with the presumed contrast: to scientificity or statistical certainty, which is allegedly cleansed of distortions, feelings, vested interests and other subjective elements. It is this contrast many feminist and other critics of big science, in its complicity with larger social-political-economic agendas, are engaged in interrogating.

For Karen Messing, as I have suggested, testimony is especially problematic in public- political negotiations conducted with granting agencies and research institutions (which one might plausibly see as present-day counterparts of Steven Shapin's "gentlemanly society" (1994: 42), where the epistemic reliability of gentlemen could be taken on trust). Hence, Messing notes, for example, that scientific consultants and granting agencies joined with employers to deny funding to a research team whose study was designed to rely on evidence drawn from interviews with workers, in which the consultants saw an uncontrollable source of bias. They invoked a rhetorical contrast to the scientific rigour of statistical mappings, impersonal data and controlled experiments, contending that workers "may have an ax to grind" or "will overreport exposure to whatever they think may have caused it" (1978: 67). Because the symptoms reported in interviews are not quantifiable, they were discredited before the fact for being too particular, too variable to yield the results the adjudicators required to support compensation claims. Messing also found that: "for the same researcher, grant proposals were more likely to be accepted if the project involved nonhumans or human cells in culture rather than live humans" (47). Thus referees decided against funding a study of cell mutations in radiology technicians, which was to examine live cells taken from the workers themselves, because it did *not* plan to study Chinese hamster ovary cells. Hamster cells, Messing observes, "are unlikely to furnish the answers to all our questions about the effects of working conditions on workers" (63). She is not condemning studies of hamster cells as such, but is exposing the leap of faith required to translate studies conducted in controlled isolation into conclusions about people's health in real employment situations, where the situation is a principal contributor to the symptoms. Here, the accuracy of scientific observation is not in question, but the imagined irrelevance of experiential evidence is: Messing and Carson demonstrate their reciprocal epistemic salience.

The issue, then, is about the relative positioning of testimonial and expert evidence: about how they can work together effectively, bypassing entrenched convictions that, when both are available, expert evidence must claim greater credibility, must supersede secular testimony to render it redundant. For Carson and Messing, testimony often sets inquiry in motion and functions as an ongoing corrective: it can generate precise local hypotheses, confirm or contest interim findings. Moving back and forth between testimony and science makes (interim) empirical conclusions possible. So Carson (86) recommends both looking "at some of the major control programs and learn[ing] from observers familiar with the ways of wildlife, and unbiased in favor of chemicals, just what has happened in the wake of a rain of poison falling from the skies." Messing explains her reasons for studying live human cells. Collecting experiential evidence is neither as straightforward nor as efficient as accumulating observation-based evidence in controlled laboratory experiments is imagined to be. It is untidy, oblique, slower and less direct; it is qualitatively variable. It requires ongoing evaluation of the credibility of expert and secular witnesses in ways that tend to be masked in formal, quantitative models of instantaneous verification and falsification. But in the areas of inquiry where it is appropriate, this mixed, multi-dimensional epistemological approach has much to recommend it.

Feminist Epistemology

The question remains: why would Rachel Carson be of interest to feminist epistemologists, especially given that feminists, with the notable if only occasional exception of eco-feminists, have until recently paid her scant attention; and epistemologists, virtually none at all? It is, nonetheless, from my work in feminist epistemology that I have found productive resources in her epistemic practice and in her writings. In *What Can She Know?* (Code 1991) I discuss Carson, together with Anna Brito and Barbara McClintock, as scientists who practice science in a style that, for various reasons, has had a certain feminist appeal (see Martin 1988). My purpose in *Ecological Thinking* is to develop a position continuous with this earlier work, yet one that also acknowledges that feminist epistemology in the early twenty-first century, in its engagement with particularity, diversity and the multiplicity of situation and circumstance within and among women, can no longer be conceived, as it might have been in the 1980s, as a self-contained inquiry, distinct from ethical, political and other feminist projects. With this in mind, I continue to find in Carson's thinking an invaluable resource, especially her (perhaps inadvertent) contribution to situated knowledge projects with their resistance to homogenizing, aggregating differences and their attention to particularity; and her respect for inquiry down on the ground, that is accountable to that ground. In these respects I concur with Vera Norwood (1987: 756), who discerns in Carson's practices of inquiry an overriding concern for "right" understanding, where rightness consists in respectfully constructed epistemic relations between knowing subjects and their natural environments.

As I observe in *What Can She Know?* styles of reasoning that appeal to touch, listening and engaged modes of vision are taken up, if variously, in the work of Brito (who studied lymphocytes), Carson and McClintock (who worked with maize). Each of them, again differently, engages in scientific practice marked by a form of respect that resists temptations to know primarily in order to achieve control; and each is committed, where it makes sense to do so, to enabling the "objects" of study to speak for themselves, recognizing the impossibility of achieving perfect theory neutrality, yet attempting to maintain reflexive, self-critical awareness of the implications of their investigations (Code 1991: 150–55). In recognition of an irreducible complexity in nature, each approach is non-reductive, mindful of the knowing subject's position in, and accountability to, the world she studies; practising a mode of observation that is immersed and engaged, neither manipulative, voyeuristic, nor detached, as the knowing subject in standard spectator epistemology is expected to be. Implicated in these styles is a concern to understand difference, to accord it respect, while resisting temptations to dismiss it as aberrant, theoretically disruptive or cognitively recalcitrant. Martin, for example, suggests that for hegemonic philosophy of science, "the uniqueness and complexity of individuals are viewed as problems to be overcome by science not as irreducible aspects of nature" (1988: 130). By contrast, the practice of these three scientists honours individuality and uniqueness as fully as it works toward general, theoretical understanding. It need not follow that these qualities count as evidence of or are derivative from a "natural" female/feminine nurturance or goodness, but it is vital to take note of the part they play in these investigations, as matters for ongoing analysis.

Whereas for Brito and McClintock, intimations of affection and love pervade the accounts of their relationships with their objects of study, Carson is more reserved about connectedness, and thus understandably wary of losing sight of the extent to which objects of study are separate from a researcher and resistant to a whole range of cognitive structuring. Her work is marked by a more conflicted and hence differently nuanced construction of the relationships between a natural scientist and nature from those Brito and McClintock avow. Thus Norwood notes, in some places, for Carson, "nature is described as a mother creating a home for her children," yet in other places she is more concerned with how the natural world "does not function as a home *or* household for its human children" (1987: 744). For Carson, Norwood observes, "the sea is no beloved mother, passively accepting, absorbing, and redirecting the changes her children go through… [it] is 'other' than humankind" (1987: 748). Hence while Carson's project is to eschew mechanistic thinking, and to emphasize organic interconnections between and among human beings and other forms of organic life, thereby contesting the arrogance of scientific and other epistemological projects directed toward achieving control over nature, it is also crucial in her view to realize and acknowledge the extent to which the natural world resists epistemic pattern-making: it is as important to recognize flux and surprise as to look for regularity and stasis. In complacent approaches to the world around us that value labelling and categorizing over "adequate seeing and feeling" (1987: 757), Carson discerns a reprehensible epistemological hubris.

At one time, in the era influenced by Carol Gilligan (1982) and the Mary Field Belenky collective (1986), feminists might have answered my question about why Rachel Carson would be of interest to feminists by contending that her work exemplifies valuable features of women's ways of knowing. I have resisted that label because its essentializing effects do more to impede than to enhance feminist epistemology projects. Moreover, Carson herself, who was writing her last words just as 1960s feminism was gathering momentum, stressed that she wanted to be championed for her message and her expertise, not her gender (see Lytle 2007: 240). Yet she was frequently attacked precisely because she was not a man and did not subscribe to a rational (read: dispassionate) "masculine" vision of dominion over nature (Smith 2008: 179). A less troubling variation on a related theme, illuminating both for its time and for Carson's own, is to consider what feminists now can make of Vera Norwood's (1993: 164) suggestion that "a generation of women raised to attach a great importance to their homes as… places of shelter" would have found a particular appeal in Carson's theory and practice. Given the etymological derivation of ecology from the idea of home (from the Greek: οίκος, oikos, "household"; and λόγος, logos, "knowledge"), endorsing this idea could connect Carson, if distantly, with the discourse of "women and public housekeeping" that is indebted to Jane Addams (in the late nineteenth/early twentieth centuries), and feeds into the rhetoric of the home as a haven in a heartless world as it infused the hegemonic instituted social imaginary of white, Western middle class America in the late 1950s and early 1960s. To early twenty-first-century ears, such thoughts may sound every bit as essentialist as any claim about women's ways of knowing, especially when they are heard through a renewed awareness of the oppressive and damaging implications for women of that very home. But there are ways of hearing them that take into account the shifts in the meanings and value implications that entered feminist discourse between the late nineteenth and mid-twentieth centuries: shifts toward distancing feminist thought from essentialist associations, which had not been accomplished by the time Carson was writing. Indeed, the public housekeeping rhetoric is in some sense a precursor of what, in some of its more positive instantiations, came to be called an ethic of care, and thence of certain early approaches to feminist epistemology that were its analogue, of which Sarah Ruddick's *Maternal Thinking* (1989) is one of the best-known, if most controversial, examples. But even this thought evokes equivocal associations, for some of Carson's detractors cast her supporters "as emotional housewives and crazy organic gardeners" who were irrationally opposed to scientific and economic progress (see Hazlitt 2008: 149).

There are, however, still other ways of reclaiming the positive dimensions of these associations: ways that point toward reading Carson's work through its continuities with a materialist ecological feminism such as Gwyn Kirk sketches in her essay "Standing on Solid Ground" (1997/2006). Well aware of essentialist charges against eco-feminism and of facile assumptions about women's — also essential — closeness to nature, Kirk argues persuasively that one "does not need to speculate about 'essentials' to see a clear *experiential* connection between... [certain] aspects of women's lives and their environmental activism" (2006: 503, emphasis mine). The connections that interest her are between women's socialization as caregivers across diverse cultures and multiple activities within specific cultures, and women's frequently assigned responsibilities, in many cultures, for care of the land and its resources. Emphasizing the contingency of wide-spread, gender-specific divisions of labour in which caring labour is imagined as women's biologically determined lot, Kirk resists and indeed objects to naturalizing care as essentially female. Approached thusly, from materialist genealogies of how caring labour has been allocated historically and locally and how, politically, such allocations are open to contestation and renegotiation, such non-essentializing explanations of Carson's appeal to white American women of her time acquire plausibility. (Analogous arguments could be invoked to explain some of the more contentious rhetoric I have cited with reference to Brito and McClintock.) In short, tracing continuities of concern need not require taking the further step of naturalizing or essentializing connections between Carson's work and her gender or of explaining her epistemic stance, simplistically, as a product of her gender. Yet she too was molded by the forces that made her even as she challenged them and defied them in her life and work: it would have been difficult for her to avoid them.

Still, the question persists: can it be because she was a woman that Carson's epistemic practice was as it was, that she adhered to both hard and soft knowledge-gathering practices, and worked within a science — ecology — that is cast by some of its eminent practitioners as a soft science? If such an explanation is plausible, what does it contribute to questions about the pertinence of her methods of inquiry for feminist projects? Simply attributing Carson's methodology to her gender would clearly risk explaining away its particular and wide-ranging ecological force with the charge that it was only because she was a woman that she thought, worked and acted as she did. Hence it could not readily support a case in favour of the work's larger feminist and epistemological pertinence. Nor could this suggestion suffice to show why feminist epistemology in the twenty-first century has much to learn from her methods and research-guiding principles, as I believe it does. Still more significantly, it does not address the radical subversiveness of her work, which is one of its major if also contentious accomplishments, with intricate feminist implications.

Carson's detractors, however, have revelled in just such gendered "diagnoses": a term I employ because of its proximity to pathology. Her femaleness has been used and abused to discredit, not to commend, much of what she has done even in its most orthodox scientific aspects. It has been invoked to deplore her writing style, her areas of concern, her emotional engagement with things a proper scientist would judge dispassionately. Carson's insistence on placing secular, testimonial evidence alongside more respectable scientific evidence, together with her literary style and quasi-narrative presentation especially in the earlier works and her having neither a PhD nor an official position in institutional science, figure among factors that have been invoked to undermine her work. In the 1950s and early 1960s, with variations still in evidence today (an issue to which I will return), industries marketing DDT and other pesticides counted among her most audible opponents: one advisor warned her: "you are going to be subjected to ridicule and condemnation… Facts will not stand in the way of some confirmed pest control workers and those who are receiving substantial subsidies from pesticides manufacturers" (Cottam, quoted in Lear 1977: 401). All of which leaves aside a range of egregiously sexist, insinuatingly homophobic and blatantly *ad feminam* dismissals, including a former U.S. Agriculture Secretary who wondered why a spinster was so worried about genetics, critics who dismissed her as a "hysterical female" and others, differently motivated, for whom she must surely be a communist (Lear 2002: 5). One such dismissal is worth quoting at length:

> Miss Rachel Carson's reference to the selfishness of insecticide man-
> ufacturers probably reflects her Communist sympathies, like a lot of
> our writers these days. We can live without birds and animals, but,
> as the current market slump shows, we cannot live without business.
> As for insects, isn't it just like a woman to be scared to death of a few
> little bugs! As long as we have the H-bomb everything will be OK.

As recently as March 2008, in a *Harper's* review of Brink Lindsey's book, *The Age of Abundance,* Steven Stoll observes: "Lindsey yields nothing to Rachel Carson… whose 1962 *Silent Spring* made environmentalism into a popular movement, calling the book 'overwrought,' its supporters 'zealots,' and the movement it inspired 'hysteria,' even as he acknowledges the necessity of the legislation it also inspired" (2008: 90). The issues are still alive, and fraught.

Photographic imagery reinforces these gender-specific renderings. To cite just one example, Sharon Traweek observes in her study of high energy physics that in a tradition of pictorial representations of scientists, "These scientific giants are shown from the waist up, alone in an office, or in a portrait pose which includes only their head and shoulders. The rhetoric of these images underlines the outward physical similarity of the men, their apparent social conformity… and their freedom from any particular social context" (1988: 77). By contrast, a 1962 *Life* magazine feature on Carson includes none of the standard photographs of an authoritative scientist in the laboratory, whether white-coated or not. As Michael Smith notes, Carson "was almost always photographed with her cat or sitting in the woods surrounded by children gesturing at the natural wonders of the world… photos that located her [according to one commentator] in the world of the school marm, not the world of science" (2008: 176). There are striking visual and verbal similarities to the rhetorical apparatus that presented Dr. Nancy Olivieri to the Canadian public nearly half a century later, whose rhetorical positioning I have read elsewhere, as having the indirect effect of undermining public trust in her research practice (Code 2006b). The larger issues are about how credibility plays out in the politics of knowledge; how credibility is tacitly coded masculine and how thought styles, styles of reasoning tainted with feminine associations or research projects that study the affective, experiential detail of women's workplace vulnerability cannot succeed in claiming a place within the credible or the rational, except by following its formal, disinterested dictates. Smith, for example, whose article is tellingly titled "Silence, Miss Carson" (he borrows it from an unbalanced review of *Silent Spring*), notes a "prevailing attitude" that she was "an uninformed woman who was speaking of that which she knew not. Worse, she was speaking in a man's world, the inner sanctum of masculine science in which, like the sanctuary of a strict Calvinist sect, female silence was expected" (2008: 172).

Rachel Carson's greatest triumph, all of these gender-fuelled derogatory episodes notwithstanding, was achieved in the 1963 report released by President Kennedy's Science Advisory Committee (PSAC) which declared that "elimination of the use of persistent toxic pesticides should be the goal" (Maguire 2008: 199). In its wake, more than ever before — and even as she was dying — Rachel Carson became an icon for environmentalists. Yet, again perhaps not unexpectedly, she also became a negative icon, in a different register, for environmentalism's detractors. The controversy has continued, even as efforts to combat malaria in infested countries have failed. Indeed, there are many who deplore the legislation she inspired, referring, for example, to "Rachel Carson's Ecological Genocide" in consequence of the legislation's having been instrumental in blocking the use of DDT in those regions. "DDT killed bald eagles because of its persistence in the environment. *Silent Spring* is now killing African children because of its persistence in the public mind," writes one critic (Makson 2003). The controversy continues. In Chapter Seven of their 2010 book, *Merchants of Doubt*, entitled "Denial Rides Again: The Revisionist Attack on Rachel Carson," Oreskes and Conway document the ongoing "demonizing" of Rachel Carson (217), drawing attention, among attacks too numerous to detail, to a website from a 2009 Competitive Enterprise Institute project, called rachelwaswrong.org. Quite apart from the damaging contents of the items on the site, the chastising "bad little girl" tone of naming it thus is egregiously insulting: a woman too insignificant to be referred to by her full adult name has ventured too far onto territory that should not be hers and is sternly reprimanded. Despite the iconic flavour of my presentation of Carson, I cite these examples as a reminder that it is impossible to conclude that, in the wider public gaze, Carson can be situated unequivocally on the side of the angels. This topic demands ongoing analysis and discussion.

Conclusion

I will conclude, briefly, by reading these diverse rhetorical strategies together to venture an interim response to Londa Schiebinger's (1999) question: *Has Feminism Changed Science?* where she assumes neither a hard-edged, dichotomous imagery of masculinity and femininity nor natural, unified, gendered scientific styles. She examines structural-situational factors in the culture of science and the substance of diverse scientific practices to derive complex responses to her title question. Here I offer only a brief thought in response to her title question, but the example of Rachel Carson bears out Schiebinger's claim that as more women began to enter professional science in the early twentieth century, "shedding the trappings of 'femininity'" (1999: 76) came to be a price a woman had to pay if she would be taken seriously to the extent of being accorded credibility as a scientist. Her refusal, conscious or otherwise, to shed those trappings may have contributed to Carson's extraordinary vulnerability to dismissal and trivialization. Yet, whether she did so as a proto-feminist or not, it is abundantly clear that Carson did change science, if perhaps not in the smooth, easy way she had hoped and worked toward. Even her detractors credit her with having launched the current environmental movement; even these more recent critiques of the universal ban on DDT credit her with opening lines of inquiry into issues of research ethics and scientific responsibility that had hitherto been excluded from the agendas of big science and big business. Her very subversiveness, for which I maintain she should be celebrated but which others condemn, offers a challenge to science, here cursorily aggregated, with the potential to effect significant change: a challenge to conduct scientific inquiry, to the extent that its subject matter allows, in ways that take seriously the need to engage with an informed and interested public so as to avoid claiming satisfaction for esoteric results that pose as everyone's and no one's. This shift is part of what I meant long ago, when I claimed that the impact of feminism on epistemology is to move the question "Whose knowledge are we talking about?" to a central place in inquiry (Code 1989).

I opened this discussion with a claim that Carson's legacy is impressive in its potential to unsettle the settled assumptions of an epistemological orthodoxy that sustains a conviction in the value of individual, depersonalized mastery and control, and I will conclude by suggesting three kinds of unsettling she performed. First, although it may seem surprising to us now, Carson's insistence that human beings are part of nature rather than spectators who stand apart from it, to do with it as they will, was startling in her time; second, Carson's conviction that scientists had a responsibility, which I perceive as an epistemic responsibility, to explain and communicate their work to the public (a conviction on which she consistently acted in her own work) was and still is both controversial and worthy; and third, her commitment to advocating for science, to acting as an informed and responsible advocate, introduced issues into scientific practice that, for many scientists and others, do not belong there. That controversy continues. But as I understand it, feminist epistemology now, in its most forward-looking instantiations, is working through the consequences of posing many of the questions Rachel Carson posed. These questions open out into asking not just about the provenance or the conditions or the makers of knowledge, but also about its would-be owners and their agendas, and about how epistemic advocacy can claim a respectable place on the epistemic terrain.

Note

1. This essay draws extensively from my book, *Ecological Thinking: The Politics of Epistemic Location* (New York: Oxford, 2006). Other versions of this paper have been presented at conferences and are forthcoming in other edited collections. I thank my audiences and editors for helpful comments and suggestions.

References

Belenky, Mary Field, Blythe McVicker Clinchy, Nancy Rule Goldberger, and Jill Mattuck Tarule. 1986. *Women's Ways of Knowing: The Development of Self, Voice, and Mind*. New York: Basic Books.

Cafaro, Philip. 2008 "Rachel Carson's Environmental Ethics." In Lisa H. Sideris and Kathleen Dean Moore (eds.), *Rachel Carson: Legacy and Challenge*. Albany: SUNY Press.

Carson, Rachel L. 1952. Speech, National Book Award, January 29. In the *Rachel Carson Papers*, Yale University Collection of American Literature, Beinecke Rare Book and Manuscript Library, Yale University, New Haven, CT.

___. 1956. "Biological Sciences." In *Good Reading*. New York: American Library.

____. 1962. *Silent Spring*. Boston: Houghton Mifflin.

Code, Lorraine. 1987. *Epistemic Responsibility*. Hanover, NH: University Press of New England.

___. 1989. "The Impact of Feminism on Epistemology." In Nancy Tuana (ed.), *American Philosophical Association Newsletter on Feminism and Philosophy*. Vol. 88.2: 25–29.

___. 1991. *What Can She Know? Feminist Theory and the Construction of Knowledge*. Ithaca: Cornell University Press.

___. 2006a. *Ecological Thinking: The Politics of Epistemic Location*. New York: Oxford University Press.

___. 2006b. "Images of Expertise: Women, Science and the Politics of Representation." In Bernard Lightman and Ann B. Shteir eds.), *Figuring It Out: Science, Gender, and Visual Culture*. Dartmouth: UPNE.

Gilligan, Carol. 1982. *In a Different Voice: Psychological Theory and Women's Development*. Cambridge: Harvard University Press.

Hacking, Ian. 1982. "Language, Truth, and Reason." In Martin Hollis and Steven Lukes (eds.), *Rationality and Relativism*. Cambridge: MIT Press.

Haraway, Donna J. 1991. "Situated Knowledges." In Donna J. Haraway, *Simians, Cyborgs, and Women: The Reinvention of Nature*. New York: Routledge.

Hazlett, Maril. 2008. "Science and Spirit: Struggles of the Early Rachel Carson." In Lisa Sideris and Kathleen Dean Moore (eds.), *Rachel Carson: Legacy and Challenge*. Albany: SUNY Press.

Kirk, Gwyn. 2006 [1997]. "Standing on Solid Ground: A Materialist Ecological Feminism." Reprinted in Elizabeth Hackett and Sally Haslanger (eds.), *Theorizing Feminisms: A Reader*. New York: Oxford University Press.

Kroll, Gary. 2002. "Ecology as a Subversive Subject." *Reflections: Newsletter of the Program for Ethics, Science and the Environment*. May. Department of Philosophy, Oregon State University.

Lear, Linda. 1977. *Rachel Carson: Witness for Nature*. London: Penguin.

___. 2002. "Rachel Carson's Silent Spring." *Reflections: Newsletter of the Program for Ethics, Science and the Environment* 9 (May): 2. Department of Philosophy, Oregon State University.

Lytle, Mark Hamilton. 2007. *The Gentle Subversive: Rachel Carson, Silent Spring, and the Rise of the Environmental Movement.* New York: Oxford University Press.

Maguire, Steve. 2008. "Contested Icons: Rachel Carson and DDT." In Lisa Sideris and Kathleen Dean Moore (eds.), *Rachel Carson: Legacy and Challenge.* Albany: SUNY Press.

Makson, Lisa. 2003. "Rachel Carson's Ecological Genocide." *FrontPageMagazine. com.* July 31. <www.frontpagemag.com/articles/ReadArticle.asp?ID=9169>.

Martin, Jane Roland. 1988. "Science in a Different Style." *American Philosophical Quarterly* 25, April: 129–40.

Merchant, Carolyn. 1980. *The Death of Nature: Women, Ecology, and the Scientific Revolution.* San Francisco: Harper & Row.

Messing, Karen. 1998. *One-Eyed Science: Occupational Health and Women Workers.* Philadelphia: Temple University Press.

Norwood, Vera. 1987. "The Nature of Knowing: Rachel Carson and the American Environment." *Signs: Journal of Women in Culture and Society* 12.

___. 1993. *Made from this Earth: American Women and Nature.* Chapel Hill: University of North Carolina Press.

Oreskes, Naomi, and Eric M. Conway. 2010. *Merchants of Doubt: How a Handful of Scientists Obscured the Truth on Issues from Tobacco Smoke to Global Warming.* N.Y.: Bloomsbury Press.

Ruddick, Sarah. 1989. *Maternal Thinking: Toward a Politics of Peace.* Boston: Beacon Press.

Schiebinger, Londa. 1999. *Has Feminism Changed Science?* Cambridge, MA: Harvard University Press.

Shapin, Steven. 1994. *A Social History of Truth: Civility and Science in Seventeenth-Century England.* Chicago: University of Chicago Press.

Sideris, Lisa H., and Kathleen Dean Moore (eds.). 2008. *Rachel Carson: Legacy and Challenge.* Albany: SUNY Press.

Smith, Michael. 2008. "'Silence, Miss Carson': Science, Gender, and the Reception of *Silent Spring.*" In Lisa Sideris and Kathleen Dean Moore (eds.), *Rachel Carson: Legacy and Challenge.* Albany: SUNY Press.

Stoll, Steven. 2008. "Fear of Fallowing: The specter of a No-Growth World." *Harpers Magazine* 316, 1894 (March): 88–94.

Traweek, Sharon. 1988. *Beamtimes and Lifetimes: The World of High Energy Physicists.* Cambridge, MA: Harvard University Press.